RETHINKING DISCIPLINE

RETHINKING DISCIPLINE

Conscious Parenting Strategies for Growth and Connection

Yehudis Smith, M.S.Ed.

ROCKRIDGE
PRESS

Interior and Cover Designer: Karmen Lizzul
Art Producer: Samantha Ulban
Editor: Annie Choi
Production Manager: Michael Kay
Production Editor: Melissa Edeburn

All images used under license Shutterstock.
Author photo courtesy of YBK Photography.

ISBN: Print 978-1-64739-250-5 | eBook 978-1-64739-251-2
R0

To my children: sleepless nights, doctor visits, tears, laughter, dirty diapers, snuggles, kisses, dance parties. You have taught me more over the past 10 years than I ever could have expected. I love you beyond belief. This is for you.

CONTENTS

INTRODUCTION

For as long as I can remember, I wanted to be a mother. By the time I gave birth to my first child, I had been working as a preschool teacher for a couple of years. I thought I could take on the world. My second, third, and fourth children followed quickly, and soon I was in over my head. I was bombarded with the nitty-gritty of parenting, the constant pressure to juggle the needs and wants of these little beings with my own. The revelation came quickly: Being a teacher and loving children didn't prepare me for the trials and tribulations of parenting my own children. I had a lot to learn.

As I developed as a mother, I began adapting the more traditional parenting methods that had been ingrained in me since childhood. Conscious parenting is what helped me achieve success.

Fast-forward almost a decade: I'm a mother of four children younger than 10, and I have 13 years of experience as an early childhood educator. I am currently a conscious parenting coach and educator. I've honed my craft through personal experience as a mother, extensive training in progressive parenting and educational methodologies, and earning a graduate degree in early childhood education and development. I love conscious parenting because it has made me a better parent and a better person. It works.

Over the past few years, I have successfully coached parents using the techniques and philosophy of conscious parenting. Parents raising children of all ages and developmental stages have reported improvement in their children's behaviors. They also enjoyed better relations with their children after implementing the systems and techniques in this book.

I want to congratulate you for picking up this book. It's hard to admit you need help, and the first step to positive change is being willing and receptive. Self-improvement, especially as a parent, takes an immense amount of self-awareness, honesty, and humility. I'm thrilled to have you here.

This book isn't a one-size-fits-all solution to your parenting problems. Conscious parenting isn't about snapping your fingers and transforming your life in a few hours. It's about embarking on a journey of self-discovery and learning different ways to relate to your children. This book helps make this process a little easier and gives you relatable and ready-to-implement techniques to help you become a more conscious parent.

What You'll Learn

Before we begin, here's a snapshot of what you'll learn in this book.

Getting Started with Conscious Parenting: Discover what conscious parenting is and how it differs from the philosophies and techniques of more traditional parenting methods. Learn the main tenets of conscious parenting, the reasons it's so effective, and the importance of shifting your perspective on discipline.

Step 1: Find Calm in the Heat of the Moment: Identify your biggest triggers and their origins. Understand why you experience them in response to your children's behaviors. Learn strategies for controlling your reactions and emotionally regulating yourself in times of conflict before engaging your children.

Step 2: Understand Your Child's Behavior: Learn about the concept of mistaken behavior and the most common behaviors for each developmental stage. Discover what executive functioning skills are and how to decode your children's behavior to figure out what skills they need to learn.

Step 3: Establish a Feeling of Security: Discover tools and techniques for handling negative behaviors that stem from feeling physically and emotionally unsafe and insecure. When children feel safe and calm, they are able to connect on a deeper emotional level.

Step 4: Connect Emotionally: Identify negative behaviors that may stem from unmet emotional needs, specifically feelings of invalidation, going unnoticed, or being undervalued. Learn techniques that help children feel loved and valued, which is the foundation for learning executive functioning skills.

Step 5: Solve Problems Together: Recognize when your children are ready to self-regulate and solve problems on their own. Learn how to model emotional management for your children and bolster their self-confidence so they feel equipped to tackle new challenges.

Staying Connected: Once you've learned the ins and outs of conscious parenting, use the tips to maintain a culture of conscious parenting in your home and in the outside world through continual connection and mindfulness.

How to Use This Book

Feel free to skip around to find a strategy that may work for a specific situation you're facing. Each strategy is independent of others.

If you are new to conscious parenting, however, take the time to first learn the general principles and work toward developing the strategies and skills presented in the later chapters.

Although many behavioral issues are developmentally appropriate, some may require professional help. This book isn't meant to diagnose medical conditions or be a substitute for medical advice. If you are not seeing success with the techniques presented here, you may want to consider consulting a professional.

This book is meant to be a practical guide for parents interested in conscious parenting. It is not meant to diagnose, treat, or replace medical, psychological, or therapeutic advice. Parents must use their own judgment and should seek professional support when making the best decisions for themselves and their families.

Now we're ready to start our journey together toward a more mindful relationship with our children. The first step is recognizing that there's room for growth, and you took it when you picked up this book. Let's jump in.

PART 1

GETTING STARTED WITH CONSCIOUS PARENTING

Conscious parenting is a progressive parenting philosophy that focuses on self-reflection to identify harmful beliefs and patterns and avoid passing them on to our children. Before you attempt to implement conscious parenting strategies, let's explore what it means, its key tenets, and what distinguishes it from other parenting methods. Then we'll discuss how to set realistic parenting goals before you set off on your conscious parenting journey.

What Is Conscious Parenting?

In essence, conscious parenting involves putting aside our ego and replacing it with a deep humility that allows us to understand that the only behavior we control is our own, and the only person we can change is ourselves. How we act and react as parents directly affects our relationship with our children, and their relationships with others.

The Key Ideas of Conscious Parenting

A key idea of conscious parenting is that parents' own emotional baggage affects their behavior. What we bring to the table as parents—our suitcases filled with life experiences, trauma, and perhaps a few bad or strained relationships—has shaped our personalities, strengths, weaknesses, and boiling points. As parents, we need to regulate our emotions before interacting with our children, especially in times of distress. If we haven't identified our past pain, we can overreact or lash out in inappropriate ways. Conscious parenting allows us to be aware of our mental states and prevent them from negatively affecting our relationships.

Emotional connection is a primary factor motivating a child's behavior. In conscious parenting, honoring emotional connection with your children is more important than proving your point or putting your child in his place. When a child feels disconnected from you, he may act in undesirable ways. Conscious parenting stresses that creating a climate of positive emotional connection is the foremost strategy in ensuring your child's success and harmony within your family.

Parents can support this emotional connection by following five practical steps:

1. Find calm in the heat of the moment.

2. Understand your child's behavior.

3. Establish a feeling of security.

4. Connect emotionally.

5. Teach problem-solving skills.

In conscious parenting, discipline is an important teaching tool. A conscious parent understands that the most difficult discipline moments can be an opportunity to teach our children the most important lesson: We are all human. Discipline isn't a method of punishment but rather an opportunity to teach children the appropriate tools and skills to tackle life's challenges appropriately.

Other Parenting Approaches

People use an immense array of parenting methodologies today. There is no manual for parenting, and all parents and children are vastly different, so techniques that work for some parents may not be effective for others.

Several progressive parenting approaches share some of the core values of conscious parenting.

Attachment Parenting

The attachment parenting movement, founded by Dr. William Sears, focuses mostly on a child's infancy and early childhood. Attachment parenting emphasizes the necessity of responding intuitively to your child's needs and giving constant physical and emotional attention accordingly.

Authentic Parenting

In authentic parenting, parents and children have equal status in the family and the greater community. The key tenet of authentic parenting is that parents are required to express their feelings and needs honestly, and both parent and child have the ability to teach and to learn.

Aware Parenting

Founded by Dr. Aletha Solter, aware parenting shifts the emphasis from punitive to nonpunitive methods. Aware parenting highlights each child's potential to change the world for the better.

Positive Discipline

Positive discipline, the brainchild of Dr. Jane Nelsen, teaches children to be "responsible, respectful, and resourceful members of their communities." Positive discipline is successful when there is mutual respect between parent and child and no emphasis on punishment.

Like other positive parenting approaches, conscious parenting is based on the premise that our journey to self-betterment as parents has a significant effect on our relationship with the children in our care. This journey isn't easy. The good news is that you can practice conscious parenting, and you can start right now.

What Makes Conscious Parenting Different?

Conscious parenting is different from other parenting approaches because it focuses primarily on answering the following question: How can I change myself in order to help my children be successful? By constantly working on regulating your own emotions, modeling healthy coping mechanisms, and using consequences instead of punishment to teach, you can help your child grow and develop into a healthy adult who can forge positive relationships.

Whether I'm coaching clients or having coffee with friends, one of the most common questions I hear is, "Why is there a need to revolutionize parenting? My parents raised me traditionally, and I turned out just fine." That may or may not be the case, but what isn't disputable is that the world has changed immensely over the past decade or so. Traditional parenting methods are no longer adequate.

Limits of Traditional Parenting

Traditional parenting is not a specific philosophy but rather a general method of parenting that remains popular today. Traditional parenting focuses mostly on stopping misbehavior through punitive means. It sees the parent as powerful and the child as powerless. It teaches a child to act a certain way because that is his role. There is little space for input from him. Ultimately, traditional parenting views discipline as a tool to ensure children behave appropriately no matter what, rather than a means through which to teach children new skills.

Pushing boundaries and testing the status quo are crucial in a child's quest to learn, observe, and understand the world. But today's children have a level of worldliness and autonomy unseen in previous generations. Gone are the days of forced compliance and "because I said so." The submissiveness and innocence of my childhood have been replaced with a thirst for real answers. If we don't provide sufficient explanations, our children will demand them any way they can.

If we want to have a successful and harmonious relationship with our children, we must evolve with them. The first step is acknowledging that traditional ways of parenting may not work. Surrendering to the process of self-discovery and letting go of our parenting assumptions are key to conscious parenting.

Traditional Parenting vs. Conscious Parenting

The success of conscious parenting lies behind these tenets of discipline: our focus, driving intention, methodology, and perspective on children's negative behaviors. The following table illustrates the fundamental differences between traditional and conscious parenting approaches.

	TRADITIONAL PARENTING	CONSCIOUS PARENTING
Parent's role	Authoritarian who controls the child	Facilitator who works with the child
Attitude toward misbehaviors	Misbehaviors are bad and need to be stopped	Misbehaviors represent a message from the child
Purpose of discipline	To discipline is to force compliance	To discipline is to teach life skills
What is conflict?	Conflict is negative and needs to be avoided	Conflict is an opportunity to teach and to learn

A game-changing paradigm shift occurs when you adopt a conscious parenting perspective. Let's explore the differences between conscious parenting and traditional parenting in greater detail.

Conscious Parenting Is Self-Parenting

In traditional parenting, parents focus on a child's negative behavior during disciplinary situations. When confronting the child, the parent's tone is frequently abrupt, stern, judgmental, and sometimes angry. A traditional parent might respond to her child's misbehavior with, "You should know better!" or "Stop hitting your sister. No iPad for a week!" This aggressive type of speech intends to communicate that under no circumstances is the child allowed to defend her behavior. There is a zero-tolerance policy for negative behavior and no room for discussion.

The child's reaction to traditional discipline could go one of two ways. The child could respond by submitting and becoming conditioned not to display such behaviors again. Any inner turmoil he's experiencing is repressed, often resulting in resentment, anger issues, or an inability to express his feelings in an appropriate or healthy way. Sometimes this suppressed turmoil sets the child on a path toward becoming emotionally stunted. Alternatively, the child could fight back and argue, which could trigger the parent, who grows more frustrated as the fight drags on. Usually, in this case, the duo has entered into a battle of wills or a power struggle, and nobody ends up happy or victorious.

Conscious parenting takes a drastically different approach. When a parent becomes consciously in tune with himself and his child's well-being, he understands that attempting to change a child's behavior is an exercise in futility. A conscious parent realizes he can control only his own inner emotional and psychological states. He recognizes how vital it is to identify his own emotional state and center himself before interacting with his child. Shifting the focus from the child's negative behavior to the parent's inner state is a process that may take time.

Using Conflict to Teach Skills

The driving intention behind the traditional parent's discipline is to wield control over the child. In this case, the child has a place on the totem pole firmly below the parent, and it's the parent's job to ensure the child stays there.

When a child exhibits negative behavior or creates a conflict, the traditional parent perceives it as a threat. The parent's deep fear of losing control drives her to do or say anything that will succeed in putting her child squarely back in his place. Children and parents sometimes butt heads because the driving desire of a child at any age is to gather as much control as possible.

A conscious parent, on the other hand, has a completely different perspective. The driving intention behind disciplining children is to guide them through life's challenges, teach them social-emotional skills, and build them into healthy and contributing members of society.

Discipline becomes less about who is right or wrong, or who has power or doesn't have power, and more about the role we play in our children's development into human beings who are able to reflect on their own actions. A conscious parent is more facilitator than authoritarian. Once we have fully understood that our egocentrism does more harm than good, we move into the realm of consciousness. Only then can we start teaching our children an appropriate way to handle conflict.

Modeling Appropriate Behaviors

Typical traditional parents may preach a certain mode of behavior they expect children to follow. How often have we declared expectations to our children that we have difficulty living up to? This exchange frequently turns into, "Do as I say, not as I do." I don't know about yours, but my children would never be satisfied with this answer or implication. They would likely ask, "Mommy, why am I not allowed to scream but you are?" As a traditional parent, my response would be, "I'm an adult. I can do what I want. And it's disrespectful to even ask me that in the first place!" Because this question touches on insecurity and may stem from a place of truth, I would be driven to nip the discussion in the bud. After all, traditional parenting philosophizes that it is our job as parents to direct our children's behavior without having to introspect or come to terms with our own faults.

A parent who practices conscious parenting, on the other hand, would be able to take a breath, look within, and understand that in order to teach a child a certain skill, she must practice that skill herself. Leading by example is the most effective way to teach a child a certain behavior.

Research suggests that modeling is the most successful and results-driven way to ensure a child witnesses and integrates a specific positive behavior or skill. Karen Stephens, director of the Illinois State University (ISU) Child Care Center and instructor in child development for the ISU Family and Consumer Sciences Department, finds that children who witness domestic violence in their homes are more likely to become hostile adults, whereas children who are raised in homes where parents navigate conflict through respectful and peaceful means will likely learn nonviolent problem-solving skills. Our children watch our every move and are highly attuned to how we behave. It is those behaviors, negative or positive, that our children will emulate.

Rethinking Your Child's Behavior

One of the most significant differences between traditional and conscious parenting is the perspective through which the parent interprets a child's negative behavior. We can't control our children's behaviors, just as we can't control being cut off by another car while stuck in traffic. Our children will act out, rebel, ask questions, talk out of turn, ignore rules, and experience failures throughout their development. The defining moments for us as parents aren't whether our children will behave this way, but how we will respond when they inevitably do.

Traditional-minded parents tend to interpret the above-noted behaviors as simply bad, which causes them to feel overwhelmed and frustrated. These feelings ultimately lead them to judge their children's failures. There follows a desperate desire to ensure these failures never happen again, which leads to irrational punishment. As fear of failure grows, punishments can become overblown, and parents become less able to teach children appropriate skills to handle future conflict.

Through the lens of conscious parenting, your perspective on your child's behavior shifts significantly. Instead of viewing negative behavior as bad and intentional, you recognize it as a mistake and thereby develop empathy toward your child. This awareness can help you stay centered in moments of stress.

Consequences, Not Punishment

The term *punishment* refers to something done to or inflicted on a child in order to inhibit the child from acting negatively again. Punishments are often completely unrelated to the behavior and are intended to be extremely unpleasant.

The underlying motivation of punishing a child is to prevent misbehavior from recurring, but punishment is mostly unproductive because its irrelevance does not help instruct the child about what he did wrong and why it is wrong. It also fails to teach him a skill to use next time he is in a similar scenario.

Conscious parenting throws this concept of punishment out the window. A conscious parent views misbehavior as a child's attempt to communicate a need, making punishment futile—even detrimental—in helping her communicate those needs more appropriately.

Instead, we use natural consequences that organically follow the behavior and logical consequences directly related to the challenging behavior. Both set limits while teaching children a more appropriate way to behave. Allowing children to experience the natural consequences that occur as a result of their actions is valuable. We cover these types of consequences in more depth throughout the book.

Long-Term Benefits

Conscious parenting is more than just a positive way to interact with your children. It is also a long-lasting blueprint for your ongoing relationships with your children as well as their relationships with those around them.

Because conscious parenting strengthens your introspective skills, your children will learn them, too. From watching you, they will understand how to emotionally regulate, which is one of the most valuable skills they will use throughout their lives. You will practice compassion, empathy, and forgiveness to yourself, and your children can learn those attributes from you.

Studies have shown that children who have strong connections and healthy relationships with their parents are more successful in nearly every area of their lives. Conscious parenting gives you skills to develop positive connections with your children that will push them toward success while allowing them the space to make mistakes and learn from them without shame.

Setting Appropriate Goals

I f you take away only one thing from this book, let it be this: Perfection is unattainable, especially in parenting. We know this, yet we continuously strive for it. We are inundated with seemingly perfect lives of others on social media. Influencers, celebrities, and even our peers work tirelessly to take the perfect picture with the perfect filters to erase all traces of authenticity in the inner workings of day-to-day life. Life isn't perfect, and parenting is messy. In my life, we take 100 attempts at a family picture in the hopes that maybe all my children might look at the camera at the same time. Even then, it's a toss-up.

Only once you have internalized that perfection is not the goal is it possible to set appropriate parenting goals. In fact, accepting that perfection is never a goal is the main objective in conscious parenting.

In conscious parenting, our primary parenting goal is progress. A conscious parent makes continuous effort to improve as a parent and a human being. As you go through this book, assess your personal evolution. Are you taking steps toward self-improvement and learning something new about yourself and your children? If so, you're moving in the right direction.

Self-Discipline, Not Compliance

Self-discipline encompasses a set of skills that help with both self-control and self-regulation. The motivation behind self-discipline is intrinsic. This skill set, once mastered, serves us forever.

This is in sharp contrast to compliance, an extrinsically motivated behavior that serves to appease another. In the moment, it's easy to scream or pull a misbehaving child away from a situation in order to stop the action immediately. Telling children to stop their behavior "because I said so" will probably lead to compliance. But what will happen when they are met with similar circumstances down the line? If they haven't learned and reflected on why they shouldn't behave that way or how to stop that behavior, they may be just as likely to act the same way.

As conscious parents, we have the fundamental goal of helping our children develop self-discipline so they can lead healthier, more self-sufficient lives.

Children learn best by watching their parents. By working on our own self-discipline, we are empowering our children to do the same. You'll learn how to model self-discipline by practicing emotional management and regulation and healthy inner dialogue in step 1.

Developmental Considerations

When setting parenting goals, you must take into account your child's developmental stage. It is unfair, not to mention unproductive, to expect children to live up to expectations that are not developmentally appropriate.

Sometimes it's obvious where our children fall in their development. For example, you would not expect your eight-month-old to use manners when asking for food because an eight-month-old lacks that verbal capability. Other times, however, the line between reasonable and unreasonable is blurry, and it is difficult to determine what is and isn't developmentally appropriate for your child. We'll explore the development of these skills in more depth in step 2.

When considering child development, we need to understand a child's brain from a physiological perspective. The prefrontal cortex, the part of the brain that controls judgment and critical thinking, isn't fully developed until at least age 25, with some contemporary studies asserting that development doesn't cease until well into the 30s. According to research published in the *Journal of Adolescent Health*, "The frontal lobes, home to key components of the neural circuitry underlying 'executive functions' such as planning, working memory, and impulse control, are among the last areas of the brain to mature; they may not be fully developed until halfway through the third decade of life."

If you set unrealistic and inappropriate parenting goals without understanding what your child is ready for, there may be dire consequences, including low self-esteem for your child and tension in your relationship. You will likely have to deal with more negative and challenging behaviors.

Other Factors

Other factors can affect your parenting goals, and these may require professional intervention and help. They include, but are not limited to:

- ▶ Potential undiagnosed medical conditions
- ▶ Learning and cognitive differences such as autism, attention deficit hyperactivity disorder (ADHD), or dyslexia
- ▶ Hearing impairment
- ▶ Sensory processing disorder
- ▶ Auditory processing disorder

If you feel that your child is not appropriately responding to the guidance in this book, seek professional help.

MANTRAS

I am here to teach and guide my child, not to control him.

I am a good parent, and my child is a good child. We came together for the purpose of growth and unconditional love.

Conflict is not good or bad. It is a chance to teach and learn.

▶ Conscious parenting is a progressive parenting philosophy based on the foundation of self-discipline and introspection.

▶ The key focus of conscious parenting is mastering self-discipline in order to teach it to your children.

▶ The main ideas of conscious parenting include understanding your own emotional state and your emotional connection (or lack thereof) to your child and its effects and using discipline as a tool to teach skills.

▶ Traditional discipline views compliance as a goal and the parent as an authoritarian figure.

▶ Let go of the unattainable idea of perfection.

▶ Avoid focusing on compliance, consider your child's developmental stage, and recognize when to seek professional advice.

REFLECT

▶ What parenting difficulty is driving you to pursue conscious parenting?

▶ What challenging behavior makes you lose control?

▶ What do you fear people will say about you as a parent?

▶ What qualities do you admire in other parents?

PART 2

A STEP-BY-STEP GUIDE TO CONSCIOUS PARENTING

Find Calm in the Heat of the Moment

We all know how it feels to be in the heat of a discipline situation: Our body temperature rises, sweat beads develop on our noses, our hearts pound, and panic sets in. We see red. But when our emotions are most triggered, we need to regulate ourselves before we try to discipline our children. This chapter covers how to practice self-regulation even in the most difficult moments so you can maintain respectful communication and achieve your parenting goal. You'll start by identifying your biggest triggers and learning what to do instead of reacting to those triggers.

What Is a Trigger?

A few years ago, I walked into the bathroom and found that my son had made a complete mess. There was a flood of running water with soap, toothpaste, and bubbles everywhere. I was angry, frustrated, and extremely disappointed. As if having an out-of-body experience,

I watched myself react as my prefrontal lobe, the area of my brain controlling rational thought, shut down. Later, I couldn't believe the words that came out of my mouth:

"How could you do this?"

"But you know better!"

"How many times have I told you ..."

"Are you trying to make my life difficult?"

"Do you have any idea how long it'll take me to clean this up?"

I was triggered. The term *trigger* has become commonplace in our culture. But what exactly is a trigger?

In the context of post-traumatic stress disorder (PTSD), a trigger is described as "sights, sounds, smells, or thoughts that remind you of the traumatic event." When a person enters into this state of being emotionally and psychologically triggered, he feels as though he's reliving the trauma. His brain stem becomes stimulated, and the brain enters what is known as survival mode and initiates the fight-or-flight response. The sympathetic nervous system takes over, and the body begins the process of ensuring its survival.

But when we're in conflict with our children, we most likely aren't experiencing real trauma. So why does our survival mode kick in? According to Dr. Carolyn Fisher, a psychologist at the Cleveland Clinic, our stress response was designed to help us survive during evolution, but it has evolved since then. Today, our fight-or-flight response can often be stimulated in response to mental or psychological distress. Clashing with our children can elicit a response in our brains and bodies that is similar to real trauma.

When this occurs, it is up to us to understand we are triggered and practice self-regulation, or the process of managing emotional reactions and impulses so we are able to bring ourselves back to a state of equilibrium and calm. We have to remind ourselves that we are safe and fight-or-flight mode is not constructive. To resolve conflict, we must access the prefrontal cortex, the area of the brain that controls executive functioning skills such as critical thinking, organization, planning, judgment, and problem solving.

Before we discuss how to bring ourselves back to equilibrium, let's explore the fears and deficiencies that lie under the surface, disguising themselves as a threat.

Identify Your Biggest Triggers

The first step in overcoming your triggers in moments of stress is identifying the cause of the trigger itself. Skipping this step and dealing with each individual instance may give you momentary relief, but it won't lead to real and lasting change. Once you can identify the source of each trigger, you can take the steps forward to work on and heal those wounds. This is a fundamental step in conscious parenting: looking inward and reflecting on the root of the trigger and what you can do to move forward. Let's explore some typical behaviors in children that can trigger strong feelings in parents.

Crying and Whining

The high-pitched tone of whining or the relentlessness of a crying fit can be distressing, especially for parents who are sensitive to emotional displays. Crying may trigger a desire to nurture and soothe, which can quickly escalate to feelings of helplessness when your child is unable or refuses to be pacified. When we fall into pits of desperation, we may cave in to our children's demands in order to stop the behavior.

Unfortunately, when we acquiesce in response to crying or whining, we are communicating that this challenging behavior can lead to their desired results. Breaking this habit is integral in creating healthy communication between parents and their children.

Aggressive Behaviors

Throwing a temper tantrum, fighting, hurling objects, and grabbing toys are common antagonistic behaviors. These actions, especially in social situations, can trigger our worry of being stigmatized. One of the biggest fears among many parents is that their children won't get along well with others. Any perception that a child is acting in an antisocial manner, especially in ways others could see as abnormal or hurtful, can trigger strong feelings of shame and disapproval.

These feelings of disgrace and social anxiety may affect our parenting. We might feel that the quickest, surest way to ensure our children interact appropriately is to yell at them to stop the behavior, send them to time-out in order to calm down, reward them for positive behavior, or punish them by taking away a toy or TV time.

If we are desperate enough, we might start to withhold love and affection from our children in an effort to change their behavior. If we don't acknowledge our deep-rooted fears, we can slip into a habit of overreacting to aggression or cutting off positive connection with our children, which will only make the behaviors worse.

Disrespectful Behaviors

Rude and disrespectful behaviors are a colossal trigger for many parents, myself included. Talking back, eye-rolling, name-calling, and the infamous "No!" are just a few behaviors that can make us want to pull out our hair or cry in the shower. These types of behaviors often make us feel undervalued. They feel threatening to our sense of self and challenge our parental authority. They drive us to want to take back our power.

Parents feel that we're constantly giving our all to our children, so when they respond with a snarky comment, it may trigger an overblown response and cause resentment. If, however, we acknowledge the trigger and identify why we are feeling triggered, we can circumvent the power struggle and dive right into what is causing our children's disrespectful behavior.

Not Listening

Nothing is more infuriating than when your children disobey you, break your rules, or ignore what you say. When experiencing moments of disobedience from your children, you might ask yourself the following: If my children hold the reins in our relationship, what am I left with? How can I maintain order in a home without control? If I don't have my children's respect, how can I be an effective parent? Feeling a loss of power is a tough pill to swallow, especially when we feel we have given it up to our children.

Whether it's a matter of ego or a feeling of vulnerability, parents who feel that their place in the family is being threatened may respond by nagging or yelling in an effort to force compliance. These techniques may do more harm than good by isolating parents from their children or instigating a battle of wills. As you'll see in step 2, most disobedient behaviors are not the result of bad intentions. Your child is usually trying to convey a deeper message, and you are less likely to hear it clearly if you overreact.

Perceived Failure

Most parents have expectations of their children: how they will act and speak, how well they will perform academically, how many friends they'll have, and sometimes even what their interests and talents will be. When we set unrealistically high expectations for our children, we are more likely to perceive failure. When our children don't live up to our expectations, our own fears of failure are triggered. Parenting can feel challenging when we believe our children are a reflection of us. We think their successes are our successes, and their failures are our failures.

When we perceive that our children have failed, we may have the following reactions:

"This can't happen to my child."

"I'm a failure if my child doesn't succeed."

"How will she get into a good school if she doesn't do well?"

"What will other people think of me?"

"I can't allow myself to fail as a parent."

These irrational reactions to your child's perceived failures will only exert unfair pressure on your child. This type of pressure can lead to more negative behavior.

What to Do When You Feel Triggered

Now that we have explored what triggers are, where they come from, and why we may experience them, let's dive into practical techniques you can use to face those triggers and center yourself so you can teach your children from a place of calm.

Dopamine and serotonin are the chemicals in the brain that help stabilize our moods and generally keep us happy and on an even keel. When we are relaxed and calm, our chemical levels are in equilibrium. In times of stress, dopamine and serotonin levels decrease to allow survival mode to kick in. The key to calming and centering yourself when you feel triggered is to encourage the production of these chemicals by any means necessary.

When You Feel Like Screaming

If you find yourself in a situation where your voice is starting to rise, pause and take deep belly breaths. This will bring you to a more grounded, focused state. Place your hand over your belly and breathe in through your nose, slowly, until you have filled your body with as much breath as possible. Keep your breath at the back of your throat for a split second, then slowly blow it out through your mouth.

You may have to do this a few times before you start to feel yourself relax. Make sure your stomach is expanding with each inhale. This type of breathing takes practice. Remember, the lessons can wait until you can communicate without yelling.

Why does this work? When your emotions are out of control, you revert to feelings of fear or inadequacy and may be tempted to react. When you breathe in deeply, the oxygen hits your brain and stimulates it to start producing dopamine and serotonin again. This has a quick calming effect. When we are in a calm state, our emotions take a back seat, and we are once again able to access our logic.

When You Start Bargaining

We try our best to communicate with our children in a healthy way. But sometimes it's just too hard to quell our frustration or anger, so we bargain with them. Before you know it, you've entered into a full-blown negotiation with your five-year-old.

Bartering consequences or rewards is a last, desperate attempt at forcing compliance and cooperation. Before you enter into a power struggle, just walk away. You may feel like you are surrendering or acquiescing, or that you've lost the game, but remember: The point is not to win over your child.

This is about hitting the reset button and preventing yourself from being sucked into a fight. It's okay to walk away. Your children will be fine. It's valuable to show them you are human and sometimes need to take a little space to reach a point where communication will be healthy. Revisit the situation when you're no longer at a boiling point and your mind is clear.

When You Assume Negative Intent

How we view the intent behind our children's behaviors directly affects how we react to them. If we believe that our children are trying to be bad, mean, frustrating, or annoying, we are assuming negative intent. This puts us in a negative place with a negative outlook.

In contrast, if we understand that behavior is an attempt to meet a particular need, we can assume positive intent and communicate with our children in a more positive, constructive way.

When you feel yourself start to assign negative intent to your child, pause and ask why. Ask yourself, "If I were a child, why would I _____?" Taking a moment to think about the situation from a child's perspective can help you understand where your child is coming from. Once you assign positive intent to the behavior, you can begin to communicate more calmly and respectfully.

When You Want to Blame Your Child

In the heat of the moment, you may be tempted to blame your child. Remember that misbehavior is an attempt at communication or a developmental rite of passage. Even when children misbehave, blaming them is futile and unfair.

In highly tense situations when it doesn't feel practical to breathe deeply, stop and count slowly and rhythmically to 10. This should feel like a slow and steady chant in your head. Doing this forces you to take some time and space to gather your thoughts before you say or think things you may regret.

Why does this work? Rhythmic chanting prompts your brain to begin producing dopamine and serotonin and calms you down. Once you've finished counting and reached a more relaxed state, you and your child have been forced to take a moment before reacting and possibly further damaging your relationship. Now you can communicate in a way that is exponentially more conducive to growth, learning, and respect. More often than not, you'll find that the original conflict resolves itself while you are counting. Once that wave of upset subsides, your rational mind understands the absurdity of casting blame on a child.

When You Feel Shame or Guilt

Conflict with your children can trigger deep feelings of guilt or shame. Misbehaviors can make us feel like failures, which sends us into a spiral of self-doubt or self-loathing. When you start to slip into this state, try to distract yourself by playing some music. Revisit the conflict once you've arrived at that calm place.

Why does this work? When you listen to music, your entire brain lights up. Music enhances the functions of the prefrontal lobe, which controls rational thought. It also stimulates the temporal lobe, also known as the language center of the brain, and increases communication skills. Like the other techniques we've explored, music stimulates the release of dopamine in the brain. It also helps lower your blood pressure and slow your heart rate, thereby reducing stress. Listening to music can pull you out of the vicious cycle of shame by allowing you to think more clearly.

When You Want to Lecture

When we feel particularly frustrated with our children's lack of compliance or disobedience, we may revert to nagging, scolding, and lecturing in the hopes that this will motivate them to obey us.

But lecturing our children leads to feelings of resentment and defensiveness. Sternly pointing out their misdeeds shames them and makes them feel as though they are bad. This approach is counterproductive in helping them learn to act appropriately because it shuts down the learning centers of their brains. A more effective way to approach your child in these moments is to ask forward-looking questions. Here are a few examples:

"How can you prevent this from happening again?"

"How can you remember to bring your book next time?"

"What can I do to help you feel better?"

Why does it work? When communicating with our children, we often ask questions that focus on the past: "Why didn't you do your homework?" or "How could you have forgotten the library book at home?" These questions focus on the past and lead us right back to where we started—a place of shame. Forward-looking questions create an open line of communication with your children and defuse the situation by asking for their input.

When You Lose Your Cool

From time to time, you will lose your composure. We all do. But when push comes to shove, our children won't remember the moments we lose control as much as how we fix those moments. If you lose your composure, let some time pass. Once you feel calm enough, approach your child and say this:

Revisit: "I know we had a tough time communicating before."

Calmly start a discussion. Because you made the first move, your child will be more receptive to talking about the conflict.

Validate: "I was upset and so were you, so we may have said things we didn't mean."

Acknowledge earlier words and behavior without shaming either party. Teach your child to be accountable for her words or actions by being accountable yourself.

Repair: "Let's try again."

Wipe the slate clean and begin to repair any damage.

If your child is not receptive, you can say, "I see you're still upset and you're not ready to talk about this yet. I want you to know that I love you, and whenever you're ready, I'm here." Allow your child to approach you in her own time.

RECAP

▶ Triggers initiate the fight-or-flight response, which blocks rational decision-making in favor of ensuring survival.

▶ The prefrontal cortex of the brain controls critical thinking, judgment, and problem-solving skills.

▶ Feelings of embarrassment, helplessness, and failure and the threat of loss of control are common triggers that cloud our judgment.

▶ Dopamine and serotonin are hormones in the brain that produce feelings of calm, mood stability, and harmony.

▶ When the fight-or-flight response kicks in, dopamine and serotonin production is blocked.

- Belly breathing, counting slowly, listening to music, asking forward-looking questions, and assuming positive intent are effective ways to remain calm during conflict.

- When you lose composure, revisit the situation and repair the relationship by admitting your mistakes.

REFLECT

- What are your biggest triggers?

- In what circumstances are you most prone to being triggered?

- Which calming technique resonates most with you, and why?

Understand Your Child's Behavior

This chapter provides an overview of childhood developmental stages and common misbehaviors for each stage to help you think about your child's behaviors in a larger developmental context. You'll learn about the concept of mistaken behaviors to reframe what we typically think of as bad behaviors. You'll see how executive functioning skills affect parenting and how you can help model those skills. It's not easy to evaluate your child's behavior objectively while he is in the middle of a temper tantrum, but it's important to accurately assess it before you try anything else. You'll also gain tools to help assess why your child might be behaving a certain way.

SELF-CHECK

Before you engage with your child, ask yourself: Am I calm? Do I feel flustered or frustrated? It's okay to return to step 1 to reach a level of mindfulness so you are fully equipped with the right tools to engage your child appropriately. If you're feeling centered, let's proceed.

Misbehavior vs. Mistaken Behavior

There is an important distinction between misbehavior and mistaken behavior. Understanding this difference has been extremely helpful in my own conscious parenting journey. Looking at what is driving negative behavior can provide a different mindset with which to approach your children.

Dr. Dan Gartrell, an early childhood educator, explains that thinking of misbehaviors as mistaken behaviors prevents us from assuming negative intent in the child. We can start to see misbehaviors "as an error in judgment that may cause or contribute to a conflict," rather than a character flaw. When we remind ourselves that children make mistakes because they still have so much to learn, we can start to be more patient and understanding.

This semantic distinction is important because our mindset dictates how we interpret and respond to our children's behaviors. Understanding the subtle difference between misbehavior and mistaken behavior is vital in helping us transform our viewpoint. The following table summarizes the key differences between misbehavior and mistaken behavior.

MISBEHAVIOR	MISTAKEN BEHAVIOR
Behavior is driven by a desire to hurt or disappoint.	Behavior is driven by a desire to better navigate the world.
We are led to judge and label the child as bad.	No judgment—we understand the child is still in progress.
We become easily overwhelmed and frustrated.	We are led to be empathetic and compassionate.
We say and do things we later regret.	We are patient, kind, and understanding.
We are led to punishment in order to put children in their place.	We are led to teach the child a skill resulting in future success.

Whether a child is 2 or 16 years old, she's still discovering the world and how it works. If we view her behavior as bad, we will interpret her intentions as bad. If we interpret the intention driving the behavior as bad, we're more likely to be emotionally triggered, and nothing constructive comes from that mindset.

Children exhibit challenging behaviors because that is how they learn. We can't control this variable and we shouldn't want to, as it's a path toward healthy development. The only thing we can control is where we go from there. Ask yourself the following questions to stay focused on the objective: How can I help my child move forward? What skills can I teach my child so he can act differently next time the same scenario arises?

For the sake of convenience, this book refers to challenging behavior as "misbehavior," but I'm not using the term to interpret this challenging behavior as *bad*. Again, children's difficult behaviors are driven by mistakes in judgment and ongoing learning.

Now that we understand that children misbehave in order to grow, develop, and discover the world around them, let's take a look at some common misbehaviors during each stage of development.

Overview of Common Misbehaviors

The challenging behaviors listed under each developmental stage are general guidelines. Many behaviors can overlap across stages, but I try to match each behavior with the age group where it's most prevalent. Children also develop at different paces, so this is not a one-size-fits-all overview. Always consult a pediatrician or specialist to determine whether your child is delayed in any particular area or needs any extra support.

Toddler Misbehaviors (Ages 1 to 3)

Have you ever tried to learn a new language? Do you remember that time of transition, when you knew a few words here and there but still had to dig into your brain and translate from your native tongue? It took time and effort, and it was often frustrating.

Now, imagine this: As you became more familiar with and fluent in this new language, you stub your toe against the corner of the couch and begin to howl in pain. Do you think your cries would be in the newly learned language or your primary one? Your response would probably default to your more natural and effortless language. Why?

When our physical bodies or emotional vulnerabilities are threatened, we enter our most primal fight-or-flight mode. In these moments, we are concerned only with survival. We aren't able to access the parts of our brains that control critical thinking or retrieve new information. Instead, we access the most deeply etched, and therefore most easily retrieved, information: our natural state of being.

For young children, verbal language is like a second language. Their first language is physical. From the time they were in the womb, they communicated using their bodies. As infants, they cried, flailed, and twisted in order to communicate their needs. When they were finished eating, they pushed away the bottle or their mother's chest. When they were ready to be picked up, they waved their arms.

In many early childhood classrooms across the world, teachers use a technique known as Total Physical Response (TPR) to teach language skills to young children simultaneously through speech and physical activity. Developed by James Asher, a psychology professor at San Jose University, TPR is extremely effective because of the tight, intimate connection between physical movement and language development in early childhood. It supports the notion that a child's early development is largely centered on the physical.

This means when a toddler uses physical aggression toward you or a peer, he is likely feeling threatened, bothered, or otherwise uncomfortable, and he naturally falls back into physical communication.

The following are common misbehaviors that stem from a young toddler's desire to communicate his upset and desire to connect, as well as to assert himself and his needs.

BITING AND SCRATCHING

As upsetting as it is to receive a call from day care that your child bit another, rest assured that it's completely normal at this developmental stage. Biting or scratching occurs for a few reasons.

One possibility is that your child is teething. Biting helps ease the discomfort and pain in the gums. In addition, toddlers use their mouths to explore and discover the world around them. This is why we frequently catch them licking and sucking various objects, as well as sticking things in their mouths.

Children in this age group have limited (if any) verbal skills, so the easiest and most effective way to get a response from those around them is to bite or scratch. They may do this as if to say, "Look at me. Give me attention," or "I don't like that."

GRABBING

A young child may grab something from a peer because she wants it *now*. Young children are extremely egocentric, and their natural instinct is to ensure they get what they want. Empathy does not occur naturally. This behavior must be taught and explained over time through conflict resolution.

Young children are still learning social norms, and verbally asking for a toy does not come naturally. They have to be trained to use words instead, and this requires the caregiver's time and patience. In the meantime, your child will continue to grab the toy as long as that's the most effective way to get it.

In the context of language development, some young children grab from their peers in order to initiate social interactions. Children at this stage of development may not fully comprehend the socially acceptable ways to create relationships, but they have an inner drive to connect. They learn very quickly that when they grab a toy from a friend, they get the social interaction they're searching for. Because they're rewarded by some kind of reaction from others, they'll do it again.

TANTRUMS AND RUNNING AWAY

Toddlers throw tantrums for the same reason they run away from you: to assert control and autonomy.

As children develop further away from infancy, they absorb everything they see in the world around them. According to studies conducted at the Center on the Developing Child at Harvard University, "In the first few years of life, more than 1 million new neural connections form every second." This number increases and decreases according to how stimulated the child is, or how much he sees, hears, and experiences. In other words, by observing the world, your child is learning that he has the ability to make choices and control himself.

At this stage, the desire to control and gain autonomy is overwhelming, and running away or throwing himself on the floor gets a quick response from you. A child's greatest desire is to connect with his caregivers, and he'll do it as easily and quickly as he can.

Preschooler Misbehaviors (Ages 3 to 5)

By this age, children's language and verbal development is becoming more and more sophisticated. Their cognitive development is moving so quickly their bodies can hardly keep up. By the end of the preschool years, most children can communicate their needs verbally, and survival-driven aggressive behaviors such as biting and scratching should decrease.

However, even if children have developed verbal language skills, they may still find themselves in nerve-racking situations in which they lash out physically. This happens because they still have a deeply ingrained instinct to use their physical bodies in response to moments of upset. This will most likely decrease as they grow up, but it may continue when a child feels particularly threatened, insecure, or unsafe.

PUSHING AND HITTING

When a preschooler feels threatened, her physically aggressive response will probably take the form of pushing or hitting, rather than biting. By three years old, most toddlers become more tactile-driven and begin to use their hands to explore the world or respond to stimuli. Pushing or hitting can be used as a defense mechanism or a way to initiate contact and interaction with peers.

A couple of years ago, I had a four-year-old child in my preschool class who had recently moved to Florida from

Russia. He was fluent in Russian, even advanced in his verbal skills. But he didn't understand English, and he became frustrated when everyone around him was speaking it. In moments of distress, he pushed or hit instead of talking because he didn't have the ability to communicate with the other children. During times of play, his strong desire to connect to the children around him also led him to push. Over time, and with coaching and a mastery of the English language, his physical response decreased steadily until it was overtaken by a verbal response.

When a preschooler fails to access his verbal communication skills, whether in times of upset or play, he may revert to using his body to communicate. This is normal and developmentally appropriate.

TESTING LIMITS

I've spent time in many preschool classrooms. A rise in defiance is a major difference between the behaviors exhibited in a classroom of four-year-olds and in a classroom of two-year-olds. Two-year-olds will hold your hand when you tell them to or clean up under their seats when they finish eating snacks. They are excited to please you, and defying you hasn't yet become an option.

But around three years of age, something happens that often throws parents for a loop. All of a sudden, your child looks you square in the face and says, "No." She crosses her arms and digs in her heels, causing you to wonder where your angelic baby went.

This is a typical metamorphosis for children of this age. They have experienced enough of the world to understand that they have their own set of desires, expectations, and plans. They may stick out their tongues because they don't want to listen to what we have to say. They are testing limits to see what will happen. It feels liberating and drives them toward independence.

WHINING

Children may resort to whining for many reasons. They might be tired, hungry, frustrated, or just sick of acting like a big kid. Young children are trying to figure out how to be in the world because it's still so new to them. They may simply need your attention, and science has proven that high-pitched whining is an effective way to get it.

In a 2010 study by Rosemarie Sokol Chang and Nicholas S. Thompson, a group of adults were read stories using two different types of voices: a whiny one and a neutral one. While the adults were listening to the stories, "[they] were monitored for Galvanic skin response, heart rate, and blood pressure. Based on 4 measures, participants tuned in more to whining, and to a lesser extent child-directed speech, than neutral speech segments that served as a control." This research showed that children's whines are more effective than neutral tones of voice in getting their caregivers' attention. As annoying as it can be, whining is a perfectly typical way for children to get their needs met.

School-Age Misbehaviors (Ages 6 to 12)

As young children mature, their behaviors change significantly. But older children are still concerned with pleasing us, connecting to friends and family, creating and maintaining relationships, and developing their individuality and autonomy. All these deep desires last into adulthood.

What changes throughout child development is how children react to stimuli, navigate adversity, and defend themselves against perceived emotional or physical threats. The explanations for the next behaviors are more concise, as school-age children have a greater ability to verbally express why they act the way they do.

BAD SPORTSMANSHIP

School-age children often exhibit bad sportsmanship when participating in games or sports. Interacting with a child who storms out of the room, crying and screeching, whenever he loses a board game can be frustrating.

Not only is this stressful for everyone involved, but it is also extremely triggering for those of us who imagined our children would grow up to be good sports. A child who displays an extreme response to losing is probably feeling insecure. Children who are secure in their own accomplishments and gifts are generally gracious and don't have a hard time losing.

DEFIANCE

Defiant behaviors can include rule breaking, eye-rolling, and so on. This set of behaviors carries on throughout every stage of development. As children grow up and mature, their desire for independence increases as well. It is every human being's desire to achieve goals, create relationships, and explore the world. Children's desires may cause them to respond to us defiantly, as they want to make their own choices and live their own lives.

Alternatively, sometimes school-age children become defiant in order to communicate underlying frustration or emotional distress. Because we have created a safe place for them to land, they may release any upset they're holding through moments of defiance. As challenging as it is to face a defiant child, if you have successfully created a culture of warmth and support, the defiance may actually show that your child views you as her safe haven, and she feels free to express any grievances.

BULLYING

The biggest expectation I had for my kids, even before they were born, was that they always be kind toward others. "I'd rather my kid be bullied than be the bully," I said. Most parents would be sad and disappointed to find out their child was displaying bullying-type behaviors, and it would likely trigger feelings of failure and embarrassment.

But let's push our own feelings aside and dive deeper. Why do children bully? The answer is simple (although the solution may not be): Children who bully usually have a deep-seated desire to positively connect to others. When a child's desire to connect isn't fulfilled, she will try to remedy it in any way. Often, the result is to connect negatively by lashing out at or hurting another person. As motivational speaker Will Bowen says, "Hurt people hurt people."

Teenager Misbehaviors (Ages 13 to 19)

Raising a teenager is extremely challenging. Not only are you trying to help them develop their own personhood, achieve their goals, and navigate complicated relationships, a flood of hormones is also throwing a spoke in the wheel of progress.

Just when you feel you've reached a compromise or achieved success, a teenager's challenging behavior takes a turn, and you feel like you're back where you started. This seesaw of broken progress can feel futile. Keep in mind that many of these challenging behaviors are normal within the context of what is developmentally age appropriate.

LYING

The driving motivation for lying is usually straightforward, albeit frustrating. Teenagers lie because they have an intense push for independence and freedom. When confronted with a situation in which they have no freedom to do as they wish, they may simply lie.

Older children also may lie to avoid punishment for wrongdoing. Their lack of judgment leads them to think the consequences of lying are no worse than the alternatives. In other words, they'd rather take a chance and lie about being at a friend's house so they don't get in trouble for going to a party. Their developing brains make them blind to the fact that the consequences of going to the party (and lying about it) may actually be worse.

Conversely, teenagers can be fully aware of the potential consequences of their actions, but poor judgment and high impulsivity push them to gamble on the idea that they may be able to outwit their parents and suffer no consequences.

ARGUING OR TALKING BACK

These two behaviors stem from the same desire for freedom. Teenagers want what they want, and anything that gets in the way creates frustration that overshadows what you've taught them about respectful communication.

MOODINESS AND ATTITUDE

Moodiness can be attributed to two different causes. The first is the desire for independence and space. Your expectations may impede on your teenager's plans, and she responds with aggravation. The second reason is that her hormones fuel moods that can go hot and cold, adding to your frustration.

According to the *Harvard Health Blog*, during puberty the adolescent brain secretes an enormous amount of adrenal stress hormones, sex hormones, and growth hormones. This production significantly affects brain development in teenagers. These hormones affect the limbic system and the raphe nucleus, which is the direct source of serotonin, the chemical that regulates mood. This change in hormonal production means adolescents are constantly struggling to regulate their moods.

EMOTIONAL DETACHMENT OR RAGE

These seemingly opposite behaviors are two sides of the same coin. When teenagers experience frustration, peer conflict, or romantic entanglements or when they feel misunderstood or overwhelmed, they revert to survival mode.

As its name suggests, the fight-or-flight impulse can work one of two ways. In fight mode, teens can display angry, aggressive behaviors. In flight mode, they can withdraw and display emotional detachment. The same hormones that control mood regulation can cause strong emotional reactions like anger, rage, and withdrawal among teenagers. The influx of hormones released in the brain causes the volatility we associate with this age group.

This guide to common behaviors is here to help steer you to a place of understanding, reminding you that challenging behaviors are usually developmentally appropriate. Once you understand that, you can work on becoming a safe place for your children to land so you can work together toward success without overreacting or trying to control these behaviors.

Executive Functioning Skills

We've all heard the clichés "Mind over matter" and "Cooler heads prevail." These expressions are common because the decisions we make when we are emotional are misguided and often disastrous. An important part of conscious parenting is harnessing the power of our executive functioning skills, which can help us assess and de-escalate conflict with our children.

What Is Executive Functioning?

The Center on the Developing Child at Harvard University defines executive functioning as "the mental processes that enable us to plan, focus attention, remember instructions, and juggle multiple tasks successfully." Like an air traffic controller, our brain needs executive functioning to stay focused, practice self-control, and achieve goals. It fine-tunes over time to help us function as healthy, productive human beings.

Executive functioning skills are the set of cognitive processes we access in the prefrontal cortex part of the brain, or the polar opposite of the skills we use in fight-or-flight mode. A significant part of this skill set is the ability to regulate emotions. Tapping into our executive functioning skills allows us to manage stressful and emotional situations in a healthy way.

Children of all ages are in a process of developing executive skills. Some struggle with executive functioning more than others. Children who experience difficulties in executive function not only suffer academically but also struggle with social and emotional interactions.

The following table outlines the three categories of executive functioning skills, the definition of each, and the behavioral implications for a child who hasn't yet mastered each skill.

	WORKING MEMORY	COGNITIVE FLEXIBILITY	INHIBITORY CONTROL
Definition	The ability to retain information while connecting it to new experiences.	The ability to shift between different tasks as well as understand others' perspectives.	The ability to control impulses and speak or act appropriately.
Behavioral implications	Child isn't able to draw on past experiences in order to decide what behavior is appropriate or acceptable in a given situation or conflict.	Child may lash out because he feels stressed over a change in routine. This child may also have difficulties empathizing with peers.	Child may touch things he shouldn't, hurt people in anger, push in line, act silly at inappropriate times, and so on.

If children need to develop executive functioning skills in order to be able to handle stressful situations, parents must create a conducive environment for them to do so.

Laying the Groundwork for Executive Functioning

To develop executive functioning, children need to have relationships based on secure attachment, which gives them the freedom and space to practice healthy emotional regulation.

SECURE ATTACHMENT

From the day our children are born, we develop a bond with them based on trust. As they grow up, they experience moments of independence. How a child responds during these times of separation shows what kind of attachment style has developed between the child and the caregiver.

When children feel a secure attachment with their caregivers, they will usually respond by quickly adapting to a new environment or situation. Secure attachment helps children develop these executive functioning skills.

Secure attachment is a positive feedback loop. For example, if an infant is crying in his crib, the parent enters the room, picks up the child, soothes him, and lays him back down. In this example, the parent doesn't ignore the cries or become frantic. She is calm and collected, she responds affectionately, and she leaves.

When that happens, oxytocin is released in the infant's brain and he immediately feels comforted and calm, which helps create a healthy bond. This bond is mutually beneficial because the caregiver becomes securely attached, too, which leads to oxytocin release in her brain as well.

There are two benefits of achieving this level of secure attachment. First, parents become a safe haven of reassurance, comfort, and protection. Second, parents become better able to regulate their own emotions, allowing them to remain calm for longer periods during times of distress.

A child who feels secure attachment will typically show the following characteristics:

- A willingness to try new things
- Stronger coping skills
- Less anxiety
- Better at forming and maintaining relationships
- Strong problem-solving skills
- Less extreme reactions to distress
- Ability to separate from parents

Providing a foundation of secure attachment is the first step toward achieving emotional regulation for both child and parent. Let's examine our own capacity for emotional regulation and how to achieve it.

EMOTIONAL REGULATION

When we encounter a stressful situation, we immediately start speaking to ourselves.

During this internal dialogue, we review our life experiences, seeking out solutions to assist us in overcoming the situation at hand. In doing so, we realize we can handle the issue because we've solved similar problems. Even if we've never experienced this particular scenario, we know we have the skills to tackle it.

This kind of self-coaching takes years of practice, but we practice it regularly on a subconscious level. We can improve our self-regulation skills through deep breathing, meditation, introspection, and other exercises. The first step is becoming aware of our mental and emotional states.

Parenting with Executive Functioning Skills

Children don't yet have extensive life experience to draw from, so it's our job to model healthy emotional regulation in the face of difficulty.

Children take our cues while learning how to respond to stressful situations. They listen to how we speak to each other. They notice how we treat those less fortunate than us. They watch how we interact with waitstaff and how we react to traffic jams.

According to a study by S. E. Gathercole in the *Journal of Psychology and Psychiatry*, younger children don't have the ability to coach themselves through inner dialogue. Gathercole asserts that children do not start to develop an inner voice, or "verbal thinking," until age seven. Older children may start to develop inner dialogue, but they may have a tough time accessing this skill during stressful moments. All children, no matter their age, look to us to be their co-regulators in difficult times. This responsibility is huge. The way we help them navigate the process of emotional regulation will shape their future inner dialogue.

To help our children work through difficult emotions, we ourselves must be emotionally regulated. Steps 3 and 4 provide concrete situational tips for achieving healthy emotional regulation so you can model it for your children.

Keep in mind that no one can control his emotions perfectly. If we are hard on ourselves during the process of emotional regulation, our children will be hard on themselves. If we show ourselves compassion as we work through difficult feelings, we'll teach our kids to be kind to themselves, too.

MANTRAS

My child is still in progress—he needs my guidance.

This is mistaken behavior—she is still learning.

I choose to teach, not punish.

I will reach emotional regulation in a way that shows grace and self-forgiveness. This will teach my child how to be kind to himself.

► Most common misbehaviors are developmentally appropriate.

► Viewing our children's challenging behaviors as mistaken behavior shifts our mindset and changes how we interpret and respond to that behavior.

► Become a safe haven for children who are experiencing distress during these challenging times.

► Young children often revert to physical responses to stressful moments because it is their primary mode of communication.

► The developmentally appropriate desire for independence leads children of all ages to display challenging behaviors.

► Development of executive functioning skills is an ongoing process that will lead to healthy emotional regulation.

► We can be positive role models for our children by handling stress and difficult emotions in a healthy, self-compassionate way.

▶ Have you ever attempted to discipline an emotionally distraught child?

▶ How did it turn out, and why do you think it turned out that way?

▶ How would you approach the situation differently after reading this chapter?

Establish a Feeling of Security

Children of all ages may display negative behaviors as a result of physical discomfort, emotional insecurity, or overstimulation of the senses. Emotional and physical distress, as well as other perceived threats, can send a child into fight-or-flight mode. The next few chapters cover specific behaviors that stem from both sides of this survival stimulus as well as suggested responses. Your goal is to help kids feel physically and emotionally safe. If your child seems hungry, tired, sick, overstimulated, or otherwise visibly distressed, this is not the time to instruct or make demands.

SELF-CHECK

Before you start this chapter, ask yourself whether you're able to lead from a place of calm and emotional steadiness. If you're not there yet, it's okay. Take a moment and return to the techniques outlined in step 1.

Handling Physical Aggression

Children who are physically acting out are searching for a feeling of security that is lacking, which is driving them to misbehave in the first place. All children have excruciating moments in which they revert to their first and most natural language—physical expression, emotional withdrawal, or even total meltdown.

Although challenging, these moments are attempts to communicate. When we view them as such, we can see a path forward. Once you feel calm and grounded, help your child through her challenges while navigating her problematic behavior.

Let's go over the most common displays of physical aggression in children of all ages. I provide real-life scenarios as well as tips and techniques on how to respond in the most conscious way. Inherent in each situation is the understanding that you have already grounded yourself and are ready to tackle the situation in a calm, collected way.

Screaming

Your 10-year-old daughter, Amy, comes home from school angry. Stomping her feet, she goes straight to her room and shuts the door. When she emerges, you tell her it is her turn to set the table for dinner, a task she usually has no issue completing. She starts screaming, "Why is it always me? Why am I the only one you ever ask to do anything? It's not fair! I hate you! You're the worst mother in the whole world!" She runs up to her room and gives her door an earth-shattering slam.

Understanding Sensory Issues

Sometimes our children may lash out because they are overstimulated. A **sensory stimulus** is anything you encounter with your senses that excites neurons, which send signals to the brain.

Children of all ages take in thousands of sensory stimuli every single day. Many are new ones they're processing for the first time. This is a lot of work for the brain, and sometimes it processes the stimuli inappropriately.

When a child's senses are overwhelmed, he may not feel secure physically or emotionally and may display aggressive behavior. Before dishing out punishments, your goal should be to figure out whether the child's sensory needs are being met. This will help you get to the root of the issues causing the behavior.

Sensory processing disorder (SPD) refers to a condition in which the brain has difficulty integrating sensory information. Children with SPD may need certain accommodations and learning support. If you suspect your child has sensory needs, consult a professional.

Your first instinct would probably be to run after her and, in an intimidating voice, communicate that it is never acceptable to speak to you that way. You may even start questioning your own parenting skills: "How could I have raised a daughter who would ever speak to her mother that way?" You'll find yourself searching for all the creative and impactful ways you could punish her. After all, she's the child and you're the parent. She should know who's in charge.

This train of thought can escalate until your stress level is through the roof. Your focus, however, is misplaced. Your child's misbehavior isn't really about you, it's about her. Instead of focusing on how her outburst made you feel, it's time to pause, take a deep breath, and count to 10. Once you have calmed down, try the following technique.

MIRRORING

Reflecting a child's feelings, words, and body language back to them accurately and specifically is called mirroring. If done properly, mirroring creates an atmosphere of validation, support, and understanding, but it doesn't mean you agree with your child's behavior. This technique is best used in situations where your child may feel misunderstood, or that nobody gets her.

Before you start, keep in mind that this isn't the time to teach a lesson. This is about encouraging healthy emotional expression and self-reflection in your child.

Pause: Do not get caught up in your child's emotional roller coaster. You are here to help her through it, not hop into the cart with her.

Become a mirror: Reflect back your child's words verbatim or actions based on her behavior. Be calm, detailed, and specific.

Say, "You think I always ask you to help around the house. You don't think it's fair. You hate me. I'm the worst mother in the whole world." Make sure your voice contains no condescension or ridicule. Be sure you are not communicating that you think she's being ridiculous. Repeat her words straight back to her, like a mirror reflecting an image.

Validate: Ask your child, "Did I understand what you were telling me?" If your child answers affirmatively, move on to the next step. If she answers in the negative, try again. Reflect her body language or actions back to her.

Say, "You slammed the door hard. You're squeezing your fists." Then ask again if she thinks you understand. You may have to do this a few times before she relents and answers affirmatively.

Communicate: Now that your child feels validated and understood, she is more likely to reveal whatever deep-seated issues are at the root of her upset. Ask her, "Is there anything else?" If your child truly feels heard, she may say something like, "Yes. My friends were mean today and didn't include me in their game during recess."

Now you've gotten to the crux of the matter and can dive into whatever is really causing your child's misbehavior. You've accomplished two important goals:

First, you showed and communicated to your child that you are there for her. You're a safe haven she can fall back on with zero judgment. Second, you allowed her an open line of communication to express what is really troubling her.

Once you're sure your child is feeling heard, validated, and emotionally regulated, you can start to communicate your expectations. When she is receptive, say, "I know you were having a tough time at school. Your friends made you upset and so you came home and transferred that upset onto me. I will always be here for you. But it isn't okay to scream at me. Next time, say, 'Mom, I need a few minutes before I set the table. Is that okay?' I'll try to be as understanding as possible."

Spitting

Your three-year-old son is playing with his trains on the floor in the playroom. You tell him it's time to clean up and get ready for bed. He ignores you and continues to play. You get down on your hands and knees, look him in the eyes, and say, "Jacob, it's time to clean up NOW." Jacob's eyes fill with tears. He looks at you, sticks out his tongue, and spits right in your face.

You're absolutely furious. You never thought your child would spit in your face. He's not a baby anymore; he's three and a half years old! And that train he's holding— who bought it for his birthday? You did.

Pause. Take a second so you don't allow yourself to get tangled in a web of rage. Remember, this isn't about how upset you're feeling. This is about teaching your child appropriate communication skills going forward. *Take a deep breath and count to 10.* Once you have regulated, try the following technique.

MINDFUL DESCRIPTION

This is similar to mirroring, except you are not repeating your child's words back to him. Instead, you are intentionally describing his actions and why he may have taken them. This ensures that your child is receptive to your subsequent correction and expectation.

Describe mindfully: Make sure you are at eye level with your child. Look at him and recap what occurred, using a calm and clear voice: "You were enjoying playing with your trains so much that you got angry when I told you it was time to clean up." Now your child is listening because you didn't berate him.

Set limits: Describe your child's negative actions and your limitation: "You spat at me. Yuck! It isn't okay to spit."

Teach: Tell your child what to do next time: "If you aren't ready to clean up just yet, ask me for more time. Say, 'Mommy, can I have more time?'" Have your child repeat after you so he can learn the right words in the given context.

Repair: Offer an opportunity to fix the situation. Say, "Now my face is wet. Please get me a tissue so I can clean my face."

Note that this technique is extremely effective with younger children. Older school-age adolescents and teenagers may get annoyed with this type of dialogue facilitation.

Biting

You're in the kitchen cooking dinner when your four-year-old daughter, Anna, runs into the room, clutching her arm and crying in pain. You ask her what's wrong, and she shows you a perfectly round imprint of toddler teeth in the middle of her forearm. She explains that she was playing with a doll, and her two-year-old brother, Josh, wanted it and tried to take it from her. She pulled it back and told him she was playing with it. He leaned over and clamped down on her forearm, sending her shrieking in pain.

Like most physically aggressive behaviors in young children, especially toddlers, biting often occurs when the child is at a developmental stage in which his verbal skills are still lacking. In the heat of the moment, Josh had no words to express to his sister his desire to play with the doll, so he went with what he felt would be the most effective way of achieving his goal: He bit her.

As distressing as this behavior can seem, your goal here is not to shame your child or call too much attention to how *bad* biting is. Instead, you want to teach your child healthier ways to express himself.

FOCUS ON SOLUTIONS

In a situation like this, the solution to the problem is two-fold. First, we want to teach Josh empathy. We want him to understand how his action hurt another person, which should help reduce the behavior. Second, we want to give Josh the words to express his needs and desires.

Let's try to accomplish these two goals this way:

Listen: Approach Anna first to demonstrate you are giving attention to and empowering the person who was hurt in the scenario.

Share feelings: In front of Josh, ask Anna how she felt when Josh bit her. Have her repeat those words to him. If she has a hard time coming up with the words, guide her. This isn't a test. Say, "Anna, tell Josh that it hurt you when he bit you."

Provide solutions: Now that you have empowered Anna and given her the moral support to help her express her pain, turn to Josh. He bit Anna because he didn't have the words to express that he wanted a turn with the doll. Say to him, "Josh, do you want a turn with the doll? Say to Anna, 'Doll, please.'"

From there, you can guide both children through taking turns. The key is that they feel heard and safe. Each one learned new communication skills to help them going forward.

Hitting

Your five-year-old daughter, Sophie, has been watching TV for the past hour, and it's time to take a bath. You tell her it's time to turn off the TV. She tells you she doesn't want to yet, and you respond that she's watched enough. After you shut off the TV, Sophie screams and hits you on the arm. She's breathing heavily, and you can tell she's full of rage.

SET EXPECTATIONS

When it comes to physical aggression, it's important to set firm expectations at home. During times of calm, speak to your children about what is respectful and acceptable behavior. You may even want to create a visual chart with images to help children understand and retain you r expectations.

Be sure to name the expectations using positive language. In this particular example, include "Gentle touches," rather than "No hitting." Young children have more success when directions and expectations are clear, succinct, and easy to follow. They have a hard time processing "No" and "Don't," because too many words create confusion. You want to give them all the tools necessary to succeed, and using positive language helps them be successful.

Allow space: Say to Sophie, "You are very angry. I'll sit over here until you're ready to talk to me." If you feel she is receptive, you can encourage her to breathe deeply or even put on some music in the background to get her serotonin and dopamine pumping again.

Sophie's body language, aggression, and tone of voice clearly indicate that she cannot access her executive functioning skills. In the same way that it is ineffective for you to interact with your children while you are upset, it is counterproductive to approach your child when she is in that state.

Observe: If she was crying, has she stopped crying? Has her body relaxed? Is she still pouting or crossing her arms? Is she making eye contact? Once her body has relaxed and her crying has subsided, approach her gently and say, "You must've been really excited about that episode. It made you so angry when I turned it off."

Allow her a few seconds to respond. She may nod, say yes, or do nothing at all. If she's not listening, make eye contact. Once her eyes are locked with yours, you know she's listening.

Set limits: "You hit me when you were angry. Hitting hurts! Ouch!" Say this assertively but without too much emotion. State it as a fact.

Create visuals: If you already have an expectation chart in your home, reference it. You can even look at it together. If you don't yet have a chart, this is an opportune time to sit with your child and come up with a list of expectations. If she is involved in the process, she is more likely to adhere to the guidelines.

Teach: Don't end your discussion until you have brainstormed ideas of how she can more respectfully and appropriately express her feelings next time. Say, "It's not okay to hit if you're angry. What are some ways you can tell me you're angry without hurting me?"

The majority of physically aggressive behaviors occur at an age where children are still developing and solidifying their verbal communication skills. As you may have noticed, as children get older, their negative behaviors tend to shift from physical aggression to emotional withdrawal.

It is perfectly normal for young children to express themselves physically, but if you are experiencing physical aggression or violence from your older child or teenager, seek help from a psychologist or doctor.

Responding to Withdrawal

As children get older and mature, they usually move away from the fight side of the survival mode and focus on flight behaviors. Their emotions start to take over, and more sophisticated feelings like embarrassment, shame, or guilt begin to crop up. Those emotions may lead them away from fighting and toward withdrawal, or pulling away from people and disconnecting emotionally.

All children withdraw at some point, especially as they enter adolescence, and it ultimately lasts into adulthood. This defense mechanism helps children navigate life while experiencing the least amount of pain possible. In moments of extreme emotional turmoil or feelings of distress or upset, we want to protect ourselves and preserve our delicate emotional state at all costs.

According to Jan Kristal in *The Temperament Perspective: Working with Children's Behavioral Styles,* withdrawal may be more common in highly sensitive individuals who have a natural predisposition to height- ened reactions to stimuli, whether physical, emotional, or mental. A highly sensitive child may feel more deeply, react more emotionally intensely, and have natural empathy and compassion. If your child displays these characteristics, he may be more prone to emotional withdrawal.

Avoiding Eye Contact

Adults and children alike may avoid eye contact when feeling insecure or vulnerable. When we are reprimanding our children and they refuse to make eye contact, we may view this as a sign of defiance.

You're in your office working. You hear your two children, 13-year-old Sam and 16-year-old Hannah, yelling at each other from the other room. When you enter the living room, you see Sam looks downcast. You ask what happened, and Sam cries that he saw a book on the couch and picked it up, not realizing Hannah wasn't finished with it. When Hannah noticed Sam reading the book, she screamed at him, called him a thief, and grabbed it from his hand.

As your son is telling you this story, Hannah stands with her arms crossed. You can't see her face because she is looking at the ground, but her lips are set in a pout. When Sam resumes his story, you look at Hannah and say her name. She refuses to meet your eyes, and you even see what could be an eye roll. You take a deep breath in order to squash the slight annoyance that's creeping up.

There are many reasons Hannah may be avoiding your eyes: embarrassment or shame, frustration, annoyance, or the desire to avoid conflict altogether. This would be a perfect time to practice the mirroring strategy outlined previously.

Pause: Remind yourself that even though you may be feeling triggered by the disrespect Hannah is showing you, this isn't about you.

Describe mindfully: Reflect your child's words verbatim or actions based on her behavior. Be calm, detailed, and specific. In this case, Hannah said nothing, so you cannot mirror her words.

You can, however, describe her body language and evasion of your eyes. Say, "I see you're avoiding my eyes. You're crossing your arms and not looking in our direction. You must be really annoyed, and you don't want to talk about it."

Remember—this is extremely important—there should be no condescension or ridicule in your voice. Be sure you are not communicating that you think she's being ridiculous. Repeat her body language straight back to her like a mirror reflecting an image.

Validate: Ask, "Did I understand what you were communicating to me?" If she answers affirmatively, great. You can move on to the next step. If she answers in the negative, try again. Reflect her body language or actions back to her.

Say, "You were really upset your brother took your book when you weren't done yet, so you grabbed it out of his hands."

Communicate: Now that your child feels validated, she is more likely to reveal the issues at the root of her upset. Ask, "Is there anything else?"

It's possible there's no deep-seated issue. If that's the case, no problem. At the very least, you've broken through her withdrawal. Now you can facilitate a respectful discussion between the siblings.

If you have touched on a deeper issue, you've opened up the communication lines. Because you validated her feelings, Hannah may be more likely to confide in you. Maybe it'll still take time and she won't feel this way right away. It's still a good first step.

Resisting Touch

You're in the garage organizing some boxes when your 12-year-old daughter, Sarah, walks past you. As usual, you try to pull her in for a hug, but her body tenses. She says, "Stop it, Dad!" and wiggles away. You're stunned. She's never rejected your physical affection. You start to feel yourself get emotional, so you stop and count to 10.

OPEN COMMUNICATION

Because nothing overt sparked this lack of desire for physical closeness, it may just take time to get your relationship back to that point. In other words, if a catalyst caused this pulling away, you could try to fix it through open communication. Pre-teens commonly withdraw affection from their parents in an effort to assert their independence. If this is the case with Sarah, it likely will take more time to work itself out.

The most important thing at this point is to remember to respect your child's position. You want her to be in control of her body and how other people interact with it.

Start a dialogue: Approach her and say, "Sarah, I noticed you didn't want me to hug you earlier. Is there a reason?"

Allow space: Give her time to express her feelings without judgment. She may say, "I'm getting too old for hugs," or "I just need my space right now, Dad."

Accept: Either way, be sure your response is understanding and low-key. Although you may be heartbroken, it's important that you communicate your respect for her choices about her body and space.

You want your relationship with your children to be based on mutual respect for each other's boundaries so you can remain open for that opportunity for physical affection whenever it arises.

Hiding

Your six-year-old son, Cameron, is playing in the playroom. You venture upstairs to see how he's faring in the room by himself. When you enter, you see that he has overturned his basket of building blocks and they're all over the floor. All you keep thinking is how difficult it's going to be to fish the little pieces out of the carpet pile. You take a deep breath and count to 10. You sit next to Cameron on the floor and say, "Cameron, you need to pick up your blocks right now." He looks at you, stands up, and runs to hide in his closet.

GIVING CHOICES

Children have a deep inner desire to gain and retain as much personal power and control as possible, but they naturally don't have much control over anything. Giving children two positive choices is a win-win for both of you.

Your child feels empowered because he gets to choose his next steps. You have ensured that both available options result in the outcome you desire, so you win no matter what he chooses.

Describe mindfully: Quietly and calmly, sit or stand outside Cameron's closet. Through the door, say, "I can see you're hiding in your closet because you don't want to pick up your blocks."

Set limits: Explain concisely the negative implication of leaving blocks on the carpet. Say, "I'm worried that if you leave them on the floor, someone may hurt their feet or the blocks will get lost."

Force choice: Offer two choices that will result in Cameron's compliance in cleaning up. For example, "Cameron, you have a choice. Either you can stack the blocks into one big tower and put the tower in the basket for later, or we can count the blocks as you place them in the basket. I'll help you. What is your choice?"

Celebrate: Once Cameron has chosen and completed his task, make sure to shower him with intentional praise. Say, "Wow, Cameron! You didn't want to clean up the blocks, but look, you did it! Hooray for Cameron!"

Be sure you offer only choices that lead to the outcome you want. No matter what your child chooses, you get the result you're looking for.

Crying Easily

On your way home from school, your normally cheer-ful five-year-old, Kelly, is quieter than usual. She responds to your questions and her siblings' prod-ding and teasing with tears and incessant whining. Once you pull into the driveway, Kelly's older sister shoves past her in order to get out of the car first. This everyday occurrence pushes Kelly over the edge, and she collapses onto the ground in tears. For the next 20 minutes, she is inconsolable. Although your heart goes out to her because she is obviously upset, you can't help but feel irritated. You take a deep breath and count to 10.

It's fairly obvious that Kelly is experiencing emotional upset and is being triggered in the blink of an eye. Every moment you try to reason with her, she falls deeper into despair.

The question is what Kelly is upset about and how you can help her work through it.

SAFE SPACES

A safe space is a designated area in your home that is used for introspection and emotional regulation. The safe space is *not* a glorified time-out, so take care that it doesn't become another place to send your child when he is acting inappropriately. Your child should seek out the safe space as a haven.

A SAFE SPACE IS . . .	A SAFE SPACE IS NOT . . .
A voluntary place of peace and reprieve	A glorified time-out that serves as a consequence for a child's actions
Where children can choose to visit to self-soothe and emotionally regulate	A last resort in times of extreme stress and frustration

Be sure your children know they can go to the safe space when the world seems to be falling apart. If Kelly has a safe space, she can use it to work through her emotions at her own pace. Once she has achieved equilibrium, you can ask her if something happened at school that upset her.

Try This Strategy Instead

No technique is a one-size-fits-all solution. These suggestions may work only at certain times. Children are fluid, and so are their emotions. If anyone tries to sell you a guaranteed fix for your parenting dilemma, be skeptical.

If you're having trouble establishing a feeling of security for your children, here are some additional techniques you can try.

Logical Consequences

In the scenario where Sophie hits you for turning off the TV, we discussed the concept of establishing expectations and limitations at home by developing a visual chart and using positive language. If Sophie still hits you when you want to turn off the TV, impose logical consequences. These consequences should be a direct result of the child's behavior so they are relevant and effective, as opposed to consequences that aren't connected to the behavior.

In this particular situation, the logical consequence would be loss of TV privileges. You could say, "Sophie, if you continue to hit me when it's time for me to turn off the TV, then your body is telling me you aren't able to watch TV safely. Tomorrow, I won't turn on the TV for you because you're not acting safely when you hit me."

Logical consequences are extremely effective because the child understands them. Because the consequence logically follows the behavior, the child has not been punished for the sake of punishment but instead has learned a valuable lesson about accountability and responsibility. Giving your child an arbitrary, unrelated punishment doesn't teach her anything, except that she is powerless.

Hand Over Hand

The hand-over-hand technique works well in any situation where a younger child refuses to choose how he will go about cleaning up. When Cameron dumped his building blocks on the floor and hid in the closet, you gave him choices, which allowed him to exercise his independence and power.

If Cameron continues to refuse to clean up his blocks, try the hand-over-hand technique. The exchange might go something like this:

You: Cameron, you have a choice. Either you can stack all the blocks into a tower and put the entire tower in the basket, or you can count the pieces as you place them in the basket. I'll help you. What is your choice?

Cameron: No!

You: Cameron, I'm going to ask you one more time which choice you'd like to pick. Stacking the blocks or counting them?

Cameron: No!

You: When you say "no," you are choosing for me to help you. I will put my hand on yours, and we will clean up together. Is that what you're choosing?

Cameron: [Turns his head to the side in defiance.]

When a child refuses to clean up, calmly but firmly cover his hand with yours and pick up the toys. This is an extremely efficient deterrent because the child doesn't want you to control his body. In the future, Cameron will pick one of the initial positive choices.

Possible Signs of Self-Harm

In some cases, especially among school-age children and teenagers, common misbehaviors can coexist with self-harming behaviors, which are "forms of hurting oneself on purpose . . . as a way to release painful emotions," as defined by the Crisis Text Line.

Self-harming behaviors can include any or a combination of the following:

- Cutting the skin
- Burning the skin
- Banging the head into floors and walls
- Scratching the skin
- Carving into the skin
- Pulling out the hair
- Hitting or punching oneself

According to TeenMentalHealth.org, these are some reasons children and teenagers self-harm:

- To reduce anxiety
- To feel less sad or lonely
- To deal with anger
- To express feelings of inadequacy
- To ask for help from others
- To feel more alive through pain

If you see signs of self-harm or are concerned your child is participating in this self-destructive behavior, please get help.

For more information, visit CrisisTextLine.org.

MANTRAS

*When you feel vulnerable, I will do
my best to keep you safe.*

*I am not your enemy. I am here to help
you work through difficult feelings.*

*My job is to give you tools to succeed,
not to punish you for mistakes.*

RECAP

- ▶ When children feel unsafe, insecure, or threatened, the fight-or-flight stimulus is triggered.

- ▶ In fight mode, children can show physical aggression. This is especially true with young children, who may have difficulties communicating verbally.

- ▶ In flight mode, children can display withdrawal behaviors that vary throughout the different age groups.

- ▶ Your goal as a conscious parent is to help your children feel physically and emotionally safe and secure.

- ▶ Children are able to connect on a deeper level only when they feel safe and secure.

▸ Think of a recent parenting challenge you faced. How did you resolve it?

▸ Which technique would be most applicable to address that challenge moving forward?

▸ Does your child struggle more with withdrawal behaviors (*flight*) or physical aggression (*fight*)?

Connect Emotionally

So far, we have focused on the importance of our own emotional regulation, the many behaviors that may trigger us, and common misbehaviors across the developmental spectrum. We also explored a few reasons for some of those misbehaviors. But one of the most glaringly obvious, but difficult to recognize, factors is a lack of emotional connection between children and their caregivers. When children have meaningful relationships with and feel noticed by their parents, they act appropriately most of the time. But if they feel undervalued, isolated, or inadequate, their behavior will reflect that. This chapter teaches you how to ensure your children feel loved and respected.

SELF-CHECK

Ask yourself: Do I feel calm? Am I feeling triggered? It's vital that you are in a place of executive functioning before you attempt to connect emotionally with your child. If you're not ready to proceed, that's okay. Return to the previous steps if you need to.

Responding to Attention-Seeking Behaviors

An attention-seeking behavior is one that's likely to elicit attention or validation from other people. The behavior can be positive or negative. Negative attention-seeking behaviors include neediness, whining, talking back, name-calling, and so on.

When children seek attention by acting out, parents usually react by trying to control or stop the behavior without considering its root cause. When we don't ask ourselves why our children are looking for attention, we are treating the symptom instead of the cause. This is like putting a Band-Aid over a serious wound.

Let's explore how negative attention-seeking behaviors commonly present themselves, what drives children to act this way, and how we can respond in a loving, compassionate manner that leads to deeper emotional connection.

Clinginess and Neediness

One of the most common attention-seeking behaviors is clinginess. Step 2 covers secure attachment, or the healthy connection that develops between a child and parent based on how the parent responds in the child's time of need. Ideally, the parent gives the child an appropriate amount of affection and attention that allows the child to develop a healthy sense of self and feel secure enough to go out into the world on his own.

Here are some common reasons a child may show needy behaviors:

- A change in environment, like starting at a new school, moving to a new house, or relocating to a new city
- One or both parents are experiencing increased stress
- A new baby in the home
- A developmental stage in which clinginess takes the front seat.

Let's look at a scenario in which a child displays sudden neediness, then discuss the most constructive way to ensure the child feels emotionally supported and connected.

After sleeping through your alarm and rushing through breakfast, you've barely managed to drop off your two-year-old toddler, Asher, at day care. When you try to leave, Asher wraps his arms and legs around you and starts sobbing. You are taken by surprise because he's usually happy to separate from you. You manage to get away and go to work. Later, at home, Asher doesn't leave you alone. Whether you're trying to cook, doing laundry, or using the bathroom, he's practically hanging on you.

Toddlers are clingy when they're not feeling emotionally secure. Even though Asher has never exhibited that level of neediness before, it makes sense that he felt this way because you were a bit more preoccupied and stressed than usual. For children of all ages, morning is a vital time to lay the groundwork for a happy day. But on this particular day, you—the main source of security for Asher—were feeling insecure, and that feeling transferred to him.

RESPONDING TO CLINGINESS

Although neediness can get tiresome, it's essential to remember how real these feelings of insecurity are for our children. There are many ways you can communicate to your child that you aren't going anywhere and that you will continue to be a safe haven and source of comfort in his life. The key in conveying this message is to use a calm, gentle, and compassionate tone.

Here are some examples of language that conveys trust:

"Mommy is going to work, but I will come back afterward, and we can do something together." When your child feels insecure, address his most immediate fear of abandonment by telling him you're not leaving forever.

"I'm busy making dinner, but I can see you really need a hug. I'll sit with you for a few minutes and read you a book before I continue cooking." For toddlers, each moment of the day is significant. While we're scurrying around the kitchen, they're watching our every move. Sometimes an adult's fast pace can make them feel a little insecure. Things are moving too fast to process, and they become anxious. When your child runs up and whines for your attention, pause. Turn toward him and connect. That small moment of connection can help bring stability.

"I need to do the laundry now, but I can see that you want me. Do you want to throw the towels into the dryer for me?" Letting your child help with tasks is a relatively easy and meaningful way to give him the connection he's looking for while bolstering his self-worth by providing the opportunity to feel important. Win-win!

Take time to connect with your child. During the daily grind, your child is constantly looking to make a positive connection with you. If he doesn't find it, he will do whatever is in his control to command it.

Talking Back

All children talk back to their parents at some point. Some don't do this until adolescence, whereas others start as early as toddlerhood. Talking back, although frustrating and triggering, is a normal attention-seeking behavior.

For toddlers, talking back can be a simple "No!" For pre-teens and teens, it can manifest as anything from eye-rolling to full-blown screaming matches. Any type of misbehavior is a form of communication, and it's up to us to dig deeper and decipher what our children are attempting to tell us. No matter the age, there are many reasons children talk back:

Need for control: During the first year or so after birth, children have a strong desire to be securely attached to their parents. Around age two, children start to crave independence. Talking back is an attempt to exert control over their environment.

Desire to be heard: As children start to learn cause and effect through play and experimentation, they want to make their opinion known or create certain outcomes.

This desire can be overwhelming. Because the child is still in development, she may not know a more appropriate or respectful way to do so.

Avoidance of responsibilities: Especially among teenagers, talking back can be an attempt to avoid responsibilities. Teens learn quickly that the longer they keep arguing, the more time they waste and the more likely they'll get away with not doing their tasks.

Let's look at the next scenario to explore the best way to respond to back talk. Our goal is to reduce frustration and increase loving connection with your child.

Your 14-year-old daughter, Ashley, is in her room listening to music. There's a pile of her laundry downstairs, and you call out for her to put away her clothes. She can't hear you over the music. You go upstairs and knock on her door. When she opens it, you say, "Ashley, come downstairs and put your clothing away." Exasperated, Ashley yells back, "Mom! Don't you see I'm busy? This is so annoying! I'll do it later." She slams the door in your face.

Before we look at how to handle this situation as a conscious parent, let's first explore how *not* to handle it, and why.

REACTING TO BACK TALK

After your child closes the door, you stand there in shock for a few seconds. You feel yourself getting angry. You allow disappointment and fury to take over, and you pull the door wide open. You shout, "Don't you ever talk to me that way!" or "How dare you use that tone of voice? You'd better show some respect!"

More often than not, emotional reactions beget similar ones from your child. When children respond the way Ashley did, they're usually trying to establish control. They are attempting, however poorly, to communicate that they're thirsty for independence.

Allowing yourself to get emotional and scream further ignites their desire for control. You both end up angry and disappointed. You cannot control your child's words any more than you can control the weather. You can only control your own response.

RESPONDING TO BACK TALK

Here's a step-by-step guide to responding to your child's back talk, as opposed to reacting to it.

Surrender: Accept that your child spoke to you this way, and understand it is normal, albeit disappointing and upsetting. This doesn't mean you approve of the behavior. It just means that you accept that it happened and you can't control it. Once you've relinquished this false sense of power, you can move forward calmly and effectively as a conscious parent.

Validate: Reflect back your child's feelings by calmly and assertively saying, "I see you're busy and you want to finish what you're doing before you come downstairs to get your clothes."

Teach: Instruct your child that disrespect won't give her the result she's looking for. Disrespectful speech stems from a deep desire for control, and for you to acknowledge this desire. By responding in kind, you're teaching your child that she can get the attention she wants by speaking rudely.

Instead, follow your validation with, "If you want to be given that independence to come down when you're ready, you're welcome to speak to me about it in a respectful way. Yelling at me is not okay." Assure her that when she is ready to communicate in a calm and appropriate way, you'll be waiting.

Allow space: Leave the room to give both of you a few minutes to regulate emotionally and reach a place of executive functioning. Allow a few minutes for your child to approach you. The actual amount of time is arbitrary and depends on your time constraints. But what should you do if she doesn't approach you after some time?

Revisit: Approach her in a calm, kind manner. Ask if she's ready to discuss what happened. If she begins to talk, listen with few to no words. Make eye contact and use physical touch if she is receptive. Once she has finished explaining her position, nod and repeat it back to her.

Then make your expectations clear by stating the following: "I get that you are in the middle of something and don't want to stop. It's now six thirty. You can finish what you're doing, but your laundry must be put away by seven."

Name-Calling

Name-calling, although relatively common, is an attention-seeking behavior that can cut like a knife. If your toddler calls you "poopy face," you may be tempted to giggle under your breath, but that changes drastically when expletives are flying out of your teenager's mouth.

Before we dive into the techniques that can help us interact with our children in this situation, let's understand why children engage in name-calling.

Negative self-worth: Children often lash out verbally when they are feeling bad about themselves. They are more likely to attack those closest to them, like family and friends. Being your children's safe haven is a double-edged sword: You are a soft place to land when they're upset, but they may also use you as a punching bag when frustrated because they feel comfortable enough to express those feelings in front of you.

Inability to control anger: Your child may resort to name-calling because he can't express his anger in appropriate ways. Whether your child is a toddler or a teenager, remember the prefrontal cortex that controls executive thinking and judgment isn't yet fully developed.

Desire for attention: One of the greatest motivations behind children's behavior is their desire to connect with others, even if they have to use negativity. When your children call you mean names and you react, they've successfully attracted your attention.

Let's imagine the following scenario in which your teenager calls you an inappropriate name in anger.

Brandon, your 14-year-old son, comes home from tennis practice tired and grumpy, so you decide to allow a few extra minutes of TV time before he studies for his math test tomorrow. When the allotted time ends, you tell him that it's time to turn the TV off so he can study. He says, "No, the game isn't over yet." You respond, "I gave you an extra twenty minutes. Turn it off now." Brandon looks annoyed and says, "I just want to watch the rest of the game. What the hell, Mom? You're so stupid."

This is one of those moments that can leave you feeling brokenhearted and unable to access your reasoning skills. Pause and take a deep breath. Remove yourself from the situation and wait before revisiting the conflict. The waiting time can vary, depending on your emotional state and factors like other children, phone calls, and dinner. Once you're feeling calm, approach Brandon.

ASSERTIVE LANGUAGE

When emotions are flying high, it's important to speak assertively. Assertive speech is a style of communication in which you state your opinions or needs clearly, concisely, and confidently without undermining the other person's opinions and needs.

Note how speaking assertively differs from speaking passively or aggressively:

	PASSIVE SPEECH	AGGRESSIVE SPEECH	ASSERTIVE SPEECH
Example	"I guess you can play with the toys for a few more minutes, even though I already gave you more time."	"What's wrong with you? How many times do I have to tell you time's up? Clean up now!"	"It is time to clean up. Pick up your toys and put them in this basket."
Tone	Weak; gives power away	Angry	Confident and clear
What it does	Offers choice when there should not be any	Feels like an attack	Sets limitations in a calm and clear way
End result	Creates confusion	Doesn't feel safe	Paints a clear picture of expectations

As you can see, assertive speech is the most effective manner of communicating your thoughts and feelings in a way others will be receptive to.

"I" statements are one way to assertively communicate your feelings without making your child feel defensive. They allow you to be forthright without blaming or accusing your child while expecting him to take responsibility for his own feelings. This is how to set up an "I" statement: "I feel [insert emotion] when you [describe negative actions]. I need for you to [insert desired behavior]."

RESPONDING TO NAME-CALLING

Now that we're familiar with passive, aggressive, and assertive speech, how can you use assertive speech to engage with Brandon after he's called you an unacceptable name?

Name your emotions: Although Brandon may feel indignant about his position, part of him probably just wants to be understood. Say something like, "It seems like you're really angry with me." You are communicating to him that you understand something may be upsetting him, even if his methods aren't acceptable.

Remember, this isn't about you. It's not okay for him to speak that way to you, but for the sake of your relationship, it's integral that he feels you're still on his side. (Note: You may get an eye-roll or a fresh retort. Ignore it. He just wants to hang on to his power for as long as he can.)

State your expectations: Use a clear and assertive voice so there is no room for debate or misunderstanding. Say, "Because you were really angry, you called me 'stupid.' That is not okay. Even if you're angry, it's not fair for you to call me names." Although you may be hurting deeply, say this in an unemotional voice. Use the same tone as you would when discussing the weather: calm, conversational, and clear. You may be met with more annoyance. That's okay. Even if Brandon doesn't act like he's listening, he probably is.

Teach empathy: Once you've validated Brandon's feelings and stated your expectations assertively, you can remind him that the words he uses and the things he says have a real effect on you. Sometimes teenagers, in their impulsiveness, forget they're not at the center of the universe. The same egocentrism that is natural in toddlers can resurface during their teenage years. Use "I" statements to say, "I feel really sad when you use hurtful language like 'stupid.' I need you to communicate with me in a more respectful way."

Although Brandon, like other children his age, may put up a façade that communicates that your words don't bother him, deep down he likely cares more than you think.

Breaking Rules

All children break rules, even those who feel securely attached to their parents. It's hard to come to terms with the fact that at some point your children will look you in the eye and defy you. As we discussed, rule breaking is a significant part of exploring and discovering the world and asserting control and independence.

Children who break rules to seek attention may whine or throw a tantrum when faced with certain limits. Teenagers may purposely break the rules outlined at home or in school. As upsetting and frustrating as this is, it's not a matter of *if* your child will break a rule, but *when*. You need to know how to handle this before it happens.

HOW TO HANDLE RULE BREAKING

This next scenario is focused on the teenage years because that's when breaking rules can become destructive.

After a late work meeting, you come home to an empty house. You call for your 17-year-old daughter, Rose. Earlier she asked if she could go to the movies with a boy you had never met, and you replied with a firm "No." You call her cell phone, and she doesn't pick up. Your heart rate quickens as you start to panic. You leave her a livid voice mail and sit on the couch, waiting for her return. A couple of hours later, she casually walks in. Her nonchalance triggers you, and you feel the anger building up. You take a deep breath and count to 10.

Not only has your daughter openly defied you, she also put herself in a situation that could have been dangerous. As an adult, you understand the ramifications of stranger danger, but your daughter's judgment is still under-developed. You wonder how you can impart to her the importance of following your rules, especially when there can be dire implications if she breaks them.

An effective way to tackle this conflict is twofold: open and honest discussion followed by a calm and logical consequence.

Set the stage: When Rose comes home, calmly invite her to sit down with you. You can even offer her a glass of water to help settle the air and squash any expectation that you are about to scold her.

Start a dialogue: Once you are both sitting face-to-face, start a conversation with, "I want to explain why I said you couldn't go out with this boy." Explain your fears in an honest, transparent way. You can offer personal, anecdotal support to bolster your feelings, if you have any. The key is to remain calm and keep your voice steady and even. Make eye contact. Use physical touch if she's receptive.

Listen: It's vital to allow Rose to ask questions and state her opinion. You can challenge her opinions as long as you stay calm. End this part of the discussion by declaring that you love and care for her.

Logical consequence: Now that you've had a calm and peaceful conversation about Rose's choices, say, "I'm happy we had this discussion so I could really explain to you why it's so important for you to respect and follow the rules. Because this is so serious, I am taking away your car privileges for the next two weeks. If you can't show me you're responsible enough to make mature decisions with your car, I have to take it away until you're able to try again. Let's see how the next two weeks go."

Your role is to teach your child life skills that will help her be as successful, healthy, and happy as possible. Your job is *not* to punish her for the sake of putting her in her place. It's important for Rose to feel that this was a *logical consequence* of using her car in an irresponsible way.

Embellishing Stories and Fibbing

One of the most embarrassing phases of child development is when children start to exaggerate or embellish stories. Fibbing can last for a couple of years, leading to tricky and uncomfortable situations.

WHY KIDS LIE

Depending on the developmental stage, children lie for different reasons:

Preschoolers (ages 3 to 5) make up elaborate stories because they don't quite know how to distinguish between reality and fantasy.

School-age children (ages 6 to 12) tell fibs in order to brag or gain social standing among their peers. This may be the result of low self-esteem.

Teenagers (ages 13 to 19) usually lie to cover up bad behavior or mistakes in order to avoid punishment or other negative consequences.

Although it can be uncomfortable or even mortifying to see your child fibbing and embellishing, these behaviors usually go away by preadolescence. Like everything else, some children have a harder time ridding themselves of this behavior than others. There are cases in which lying becomes habitual or pathological. This behavior is not covered in this book.

You and your five-year-old daughter, Alicia, are invited to a parent holiday party at her school. It is one of the few times all the parents have the opportunity to spend time inside the preschool classroom. While Alicia paints at the easel, you sit next to another parent and make small talk. After a few minutes, she lowers her voice, leans in, and says, "I'm really sorry to hear about your divorce. If you need anything, just let me know." She must see the look of utter shock on your face because she turns bright red and says, "I'm so sorry. My daughter told me that she heard from your daughter that you were getting a divorce."

TEACH EMPATHY

Lying, at any stage, should be handled delicately. Shaming a child for doing something developmentally appropriate is never okay, but it's essential to teach your child about the ramifications of lying and remind her about the feelings of others.

Be curious: Sit down with your child and say, "Your friend's mommy said you told Mimi that Daddy and I are going through a divorce. Is that true?" Wait for your child to respond. Maybe she heard about that concept recently and it scared her. Or maybe she made it up. Either way, be open to her response.

Explain: Tell your child that even though she may not have meant anything by it, lies can have an effect on other people: "I know you didn't mean to hurt anyone's feelings, but it embarrassed me when she mentioned it." Allow her a few seconds to let this message resonate. More than likely, she hadn't considered anyone else when telling the fib.

Teach: Instruct your child what to do in the future. "The next time you are wondering about something, talk to me about it. I'm proud of you for talking about it with me now."

Refrain from shaming or embarrassing your child. An honest conversation has more impact than a punishment.

Handling Social Difficulties

You learned about how parents can create meaningful, loving connections with children. Outside the home, however, your children thrive on quality time with their friends. Peer connection is important for your child's development. When your children aren't with their friends, they'll use cell phones and social media outlets to maintain that connection. But the deeper the desire to connect, the harder kids take it when they experience strife or conflict with friends.

Jealousy

A strong desire to connect with peers can lead to jealousy. Toddlers may be jealous of a new sibling or classmate. School-age children may experience jealousy if their best friend makes a new friend. Teenagers go through bouts of envy if the person they like starts dating someone else. How do we help our children manage these difficult feelings so they don't wreak havoc on their relationships?

Your two-year-old daughter, Olivia, is beginning to show signs of extreme jealousy toward her new baby brother. She seemed excited at the prospect, but now that he's here, she's constantly pulling the pacifier out

Connecting with Teens

Parenting teenagers can throw you for a loop. Here are some ideas to establish and maintain a strong connection with your teens:

Get personal: Make sure your teen sees you as a human being and not just her parent. Show her your drawings or poems. Share new music you discover. Even if she doesn't agree with your taste, she'll see that you are a person, not just a warm body that feeds and cares for her.

Find common ground: Establish a family football day on Sundays or pick a TV show to watch together once a week. Discuss your favorite players or characters and ask her opinion.

Respect their space: It's normal for teenagers to want to spread their wings and spend time with friends. Allow her some freedom, within reason.

Give compliments: Bolster your teen's delicate self-esteem by giving her sincere compliments.

Go for a drive: Sing songs together in the car. Talk about school, crushes, and friends. Build a connection during harmonious times.

Your main objective is to build a relationship based on trust and open communication. Teenagers will misbehave and push limits, but if your connection is strong, you're less likely to damage your relationship when conflict arises. And if you do, it will be easier to repair.

of his mouth and even slapping him. You want to be compassionate, but you're at your wit's end.

Having to share parents is one of the most traumatic changes a young toddler will experience. For Olivia's entire life, she has monopolized your attention and love. Suddenly she has a sibling who has joined her in the spotlight and she has to share you. The most helpful technique during this transition is to involve Olivia as much as possible. Here are some things you can do right away:

▶ Ask your toddler to help prepare the baby's bottle and even feed him.

▶ Give her the responsibility of choosing the baby's clothing each morning.

▶ Ask her to "read" books to the baby.

▶ Make an effort to notice positive behavior, even small gestures: "Wow, Olivia! Look how you ran to get the stuffed animal for the baby! You are such a helpful sister!"

Your toddler has been on this earth for only a few years. When you get frustrated with her behavior, remind yourself that she is trying to adjust. She will only be successful with your help.

Fights with Siblings

As a parenting coach, I am often asked, "How can I stop my children's constant bickering?" Siblings are constantly competing to get the same toy, the same book, the same food, and the same attention from their parents. Here's a scenario you may recognize.

Your seven-year-old son, Charlie, is playing with the new remote-controlled car, and your eight-year-old daughter, Becca, is watching and waiting for her turn. Suddenly you hear screaming and you find that Becca has leaned over and grabbed the controller out of Charlie's hand, pushing him off the couch in the process.

CONFLICT MEDIATION

The goal in sibling mediation is to handle this situation so both children feel validated, seen, and heard. Before you start the process, you have to know what actually occurred. Although a set of facts has been presented to you, don't automatically label either child as *victim* or *aggressor*. Instead, follow these steps:

Address the child who feels slighted: Ask Charlie to tell his side of the situation from his perspective. Listen using eye contact and without offering any judgments or asking any questions. If Becca interjects, remind her that she will have the opportunity to give her side as well.

Allow the other child to express herself: Not only does this allow you to get a fuller picture of what happened, but it also gives both children the opportunity to be heard.

Validate each child's perspective: To Charlie, you can say, "It must have been very frustrating to have your toy pulled away." To Becca, you might say, "I know it's hard to wait so long for your turn."

Set expectations: To Becca, you can say, "It's not okay to grab or push. That hurts!"

TEACH TURN-TAKING

Now that each child feels validated and is therefore more receptive to what comes next, you can teach them the value of taking turns.

Asking for a turn: Turn to Becca and say, "If you want to play with the car, ask your brother if you can have a turn when he's done." Wait for her to repeat those words to Charlie.

Responding to demand: Turn to Charlie and wait for his answer. If he says no, remind him that he needs to give her the toy only when he's finished. If he says yes, great!

Turn-taking works better than forced sharing. It allows both sides to feel equally heard and validated. That reciprocity will elicit positive behavior and interaction. Turn-taking also gives each child pressure-free time in which they have full ownership and control over the toy. Without that, they may become resentful that they aren't able to fully enjoy the toy.

Most important, turn-taking promotes true generosity, rather than forced, inauthentic kindness. When a child feels in control of deciding when he is finished with the toy, he is more likely to willingly share it.

Difficulty with Friendships

When a child resists peer relationships or exhibits a fear of getting too close to someone in his social sphere, it can indicate insecurity that might stem from emotional disconnect in his relationship with his parent. According to a study by Dr. Gerald Patterson and Dr. Marion Forgatch, children who feel subconsciously out of sync with their parents may have a hard time approaching others directly. Let's take the following scenario.

> You notice your 13-year-old daughter, Maya, has been spending less and less time with her friends. She has always been socially connected, so this is a major about-face. When you ask why, she responds, "I'm tired," or "I don't feel like it." When you ask if something happened to cause strife, she simply says no.

Use the mirroring technique you learned in step 3 to communicate that you are here to support Maya and you have a vested interest in repairing whatever is broken between you. Your only objective is to reflect Maya's words and body language without judgment or interpretation. Once she feels secure enough, she may open up more. Or maybe she won't. But at the very least, you are one step closer to regaining that connection you may have inadvertently lost.

Social Exclusion and Bullying

When my toddler was getting ready to enter kindergarten, I wondered what her future schoolmates would be like. Whenever the topic of bullying came up, I thought that although it would be devastating to learn that others had bullied my daughter, I would be even more heartbroken if I found out she was bullying others. I never wanted my child to be a bully because that would mean she was not only acting cruelly to others but also feeling empty inside.

Research conducted by Dr. Marion Wallace suggests that low self-esteem is often a driving force behind bullying behavior.

Consider the following dreaded scenario.

You get a call from the school principal, who says your 13-year-old son, Adam, has been picking on another child at school. The principal says this isn't an isolated event and she has warned Adam a few times to stop this behavior. Because he has continued, she had no choice but to contact you.

Most parents would be mortified to receive a call like this. But remember: Conscious parenting is about going beyond what's happening on the surface so you can decipher the underlying issue driving the behavior. Your ultimate goal is to teach your children skills they are lacking so they can make better decisions.

POSSIBLE CAUSES OF BULLYING BEHAVIOR

Before we attempt to fix the problem, let's review what may be causing the behavior in the first place:

Low self-worth: People of all ages who have low self-worth often try to strengthen their self-esteem by tearing other people down.

Hurt people hurt people: Children who are hurting deeply tend to hurt others. Misery loves company, and they can regain the control they've lost through hurtful behavior and controlling others' reactions.

Lack of emotional connection: This void leads to eliciting a connection any way possible. Children will take a negative connection over no connection.

Peer pressure: A child's desire to fit in may drive her to act in a cruel way in order to be a part of the crowd.

So what can you do if your child is bullying others?

RESPONDING TO BULLYING BEHAVIOR

Here's how to respond if you suspect your child may be bullying others:

Start a dialogue: Stay calm and collected. Look at your child and say, "I got a call from the principal today and this is what she told me." Let your child know you are concerned about him.

Invoke empathy: Ask your child if he can remember a time when he felt excluded or badly treated. Ask how he felt. This reminds your child that his words and actions have an impact on others.

Set expectations: When it comes to bullying behavior, you must set limits. Tell your child, "I know you're a good person, and you have so many strengths. When you act this way, you're ignoring those strengths and hurting others in the process, and that's not okay."

Give a meaningful consequence: Follow up with a consequence that is directly connected to the bullying. For example, "This behavior seems to be happening after school during drama club. You're showing me with your poor choices that you have to come home directly from school until this behavior changes."

Teach accountability: Communicate to your child that all mistakes require fixing, even if we grow from them. Brainstorm about how he can rectify the pain he caused (for example, saying or writing an apology or inviting the peer to play).

Try not to respond with anger. If your child is engaging in bullying behavior, most likely something is going on beneath the surface that he is already having a tough time expressing. Shaming and belittling can cause him to withdraw even more and continue expressing his feelings in an inappropriate, unhealthy, or aggressive way.

WHEN YOUR CHILD IS BEING BULLIED

It's excruciating to discover your child has been bullied. The effects of bullying can be damaging, so it's critical to restore your child's self-esteem.

First, listen: Ask your child what's been going on, then just listen. When she has finished speaking, repeat back what she said without judgment or interpretation.

Focus on your child's needs: It's imperative that you don't allow your own insecurities or personal experiences to blind you or make you hysterical. Your child needs to lean on your calm strength right now.

Praise your child: Celebrate your child for opening up and telling you what happened. Be sure to say, "I believe you" at least once when she has finished speaking. Add, "I'm so proud that you came to me and told me all this." Many victims of bullying are ashamed or embarrassed. Praising her courage puts you on the road to helping her repair her broken self-esteem.

Solve the problem together: Ask your child how she wants to move forward, and be receptive to her ideas. Your solidarity will give her the strength to tackle this challenge. She will likely come up with astute strategies to better the situation.

Your anger and frustration with the situation may tempt you to ask your child why she let this happen. Asking why is not helpful, however, and may make her feel more isolated. It's vital that you give your child the appropriate tools to feel empowered, not further victimized.

Try This Strategy Instead

If you're having difficulties establishing and strengthening an emotional connection with your child using the techniques presented in this chapter, here are a few more methods you can try.

Unconditional Compassion

Sometimes all our children need is our compassion. We can get so caught up in teaching them the appropriate ways to behave that we forget to give them unconditional love and connection. When all else fails and you feel like nothing is working, take a step back and just be there for them.

Here are some examples of compassionate language:

"I see you're having a really hard time—I'm here."

"What you did wasn't okay, but we can talk about it another time. For now, let's just spend some time together."

"It must be so difficult when your friend is unkind to you. Can you tell me more about it?"

"Thank you for talking to me. I'll always be here to listen."

You may have to set aside your own emotions and parenting agenda to do this, but it's worth it. Showing compassion may not solve the problem at hand, but it will repair and reinforce your bond with your children, making them more receptive to your guidance.

Create a Family Safe Space

As we discussed, a safe space is a designated place for a child to retreat to when he is feeling emotionally sensitive. A family safe space is slightly different. It doesn't have to be a designated area, but can exist wherever you and your children are.

When you're in the middle of an argument with your child and it's starting to drag on, pause. Put your hand up to stop the negative interactions and tell your child you're going to your family safe space.

Encouraging Empathy

Conflict can be an opportunity for learning. Socially aggressive behaviors may be painful to experience, but there is much to learn from these experiences. How can we teach a child to stand up for herself and, at the same time, have compassion for the person who's hurting her? Use these statements to guide your child:

"You are strong. You have value. Nobody can take that away from you."

"Everyone is living a life you don't know or understand."

"You can change nobody but yourself."

"Choose to have compassion."

Talk to your children about why others might behave in unkind ways. Just like we've learned to recognize the root causes of our children's misbehaviors, we can start to teach them to be more perceptive about other people's behaviors instead of labeling them as bad.

Teach your children that there's tremendous strength in extending kindness and empathy to another, even if that person has wronged them.

When you're in that space, you must push aside any argument. It's hugely meaningful to give your child this instant connection at a moment when she is feeling isolated. Not only does it prevent your child from feeling attacked, but it also recharges her so when you do return to the discussion, you're both feeling more positive.

Always revisit the conflict afterward so your child doesn't start thinking that going to the family safe space means avoiding responsibilities.

MANTRAS

Children need loving emotional connection no matter what. I will be that connection.

There is always an opportunity to have empathy. I will be compassionate.

Conflict is an opportunity to teach. I am here to help my child learn.

RECAP

▸ One of the most common causes of misbehavior in children is a lack of emotional connection between them and their parents or friends.

▸ Many negative attention-seeking behaviors stem from a desire to be independent.

▸ Every child will display these behaviors at one point or another. It's not a sign of poor parenting.

▶ Even children with secure attachment test limits. This is a normal part of child development.

▶ A child's desire to connect to peers and feel a sense of belonging is extremely strong. When that desire isn't fulfilled, it can lead to social aggression.

▶ There is always an opportunity to extend empathy and kindness to your children.

REFLECT

▶ Have you ever helped your child through a social difficulty? Looking back, would any of these methods have helped?

▶ Does your child become withdrawn or aggressive when feeling emotionally disconnected?

▶ How do you feel about using assertive language moving forward to set expectations?

Solve Problems Together

Congratulations. You've learned many ways to center yourself during difficult moments and to make your child feel emotionally safe throughout the process. Now let's take it a step further. How can we guide children who are starting to regulate their own emotions and seek solutions to their own problems? How can we continue to coach our children to become more self-sufficient and flexible? This chapter provides concrete tips for improving your children's executive functioning skills, as introduced in step 2. You'll learn how to help your children practice self-control, set goals, and resolve conflicts. Your goal as a conscious parent is to remind your children that they are capable of tackling new challenges on their own.

SELF-CHECK

Here's a gentle reminder to check your emotional state: Are you feeling calm? It's okay if you're not ready to move forward. If you don't feel ready, you can always return to the previous steps in order to regain composure.

Fostering Self-Awareness

Children need to become aware of their own executive functioning in order to improve their emotional-regulation and problem-solving skills. Let's explore how parents can provide opportunities to practice self-control and self-awareness.

Remember, your children are still learning. As their prefrontal cortexes continue to develop, they become more aware of their impulses and start to understand what triggers them. Their judgment improves, and their critical thinking skills mature. Although you'll notice them making strides each day, they still have a long way to go until they are fully developed. Show compassion when they make mistakes.

Forgetfulness

Parents often feel like they are constantly reminding their children to fulfill their responsibilities or meet adults' expectations. Toddlers, preschoolers, and even elementary school students may forget to do things because they have so much to remember. Even tasks that adults might take for granted are extras that children have to recall.

Young children, for example, spend their whole days trying to remember what they've been told: Brush your teeth, get dressed, don't burp, wash your hands, do your homework. When their brains get overloaded with too much information or responsibilities, they may forget some of these expectations. They're not trying to fail. They have a hard time processing all the information. As children get older, they may forget tasks because of stress or pressure they feel at home, at school, or in the social spectrum. No matter the cause, forgetfulness is a challenge to most children at one point or another.

For example, your teenager may forget to wear his retainer after getting his braces off. Your toddler may forget to flush the toilet after being potty-trained, even though you've reminded him repeatedly. Both scenarios are frustrating for a parent who has to flush the toilet constantly or who paid an immense amount of money for braces.

HANDLING FORGETFULNESS

Here are some effective ways to coach your child and help him work on his forgetfulness.

Be curious: Ask without judgment, "Why do you think you keep forgetting to wear your retainer?" If he doesn't have an answer, offer, "Do you feel overwhelmed? Are you so tired when you get into bed that you forget?"

Ask your toddler a similar question, but tweak your words. Say, "Oh no! I see you didn't flush the toilet. Did you forget?"

Acknowledge feelings: Say to your teen, "That must be frustrating. It's hard to remember so many things." Say to your toddler, "It's so hard to remember to flush every single time." Show empathy for your child's struggle.

Brainstorm together: Encourage your child to brainstorm some ideas of how he could remember these tasks. Say to your teen, "I'd love to hear your ideas about how you can remember to wear your retainer." Prompt your toddler, "Hmm, I wonder how we can help you remember to flush the toilet?"

TRY THIS STRATEGY INSTEAD

If your child has difficulty coming up with ideas on his own, boost his confidence to inspire him. Say to your teen, "I have no doubt you can come up with an amazing plan to help remind you. Here's a notepad. Write down two or three ideas and let me know what you come up with." Giving children a specific number to aim for can help keep them on track.

This method is effective for toddlers, too, but they will need you to stay physically present to keep them focused and on task. Suggest that you come up with a plan together. Instead of writing ideas on paper, develop a visual reminder chart or schedule. When your child is involved in the process, it becomes relevant and concrete to him. This encourages accountability. Toddlers are usually excited to follow a schedule they helped develop.

Not Thinking through Consequences

As infants develop an understanding of cause and effect, they learn that if they push the button on the toy, music will play. But full comprehension of the consequences of their actions doesn't develop until ages three to five. Because young children are egocentric, their desire to get what they want overshadows considerations of how their behavior might affect someone else.

For toddlers, the main objective is to remind them of consequences repeatedly. For example, if a child reaches for a hot iron, he may not understand that he will get burned. We must be there to say continually, "No! The iron is hot. Ouch!" until he begins to internalize that consequence.

When responding to your child's behavior, be concise and calm. Sometimes toddlers may repeat negative behavior to elicit a reaction. Perhaps your toddler reaches for the hot stove just to get a rise out of you.

Consider the following common scenarios:

Your pre-teen refuses to stop watching TV when she has to study for a math test.

Your toddler constantly throws food on the floor when she's not interested in eating it.

TEACHING CONSEQUENCES

For older children who begin to understand that their choices have consequences, we can transition from the role of guardian to facilitator. For toddlers, the goal is to teach them what the consequences are.

Show empathy: Validate your pre-teen's feelings. Say, "I know you have a lot of schoolwork and sometimes you just want to relax." To a toddler, you can say, "I see you didn't like the corn, so you threw it on the floor."

Discuss potential consequences: Say to your pre-teen, "I know you're stressed, but how do you think you'll do on your test if you don't study?" Say to your toddler, animatedly, "What do you think will happen if I step on the corn?" These questions help focus your child, at either age, on the potential direct consequences of her actions.

Brainstorm together: Encourage your child to come up with some ideas for how she could change this behavior to produce a more favorable outcome. Say to your pre-teen, "How can you work your schedule so that you have more downtime and still have the opportunity to study for your test?" Ask your toddler, "What can you do if you don't like the corn?" Respond enthusiastically to any positive input.

Boost your child's confidence: Encourage her ability to plan her own life appropriately. Say, "You're old enough now to come up with your own schedule that includes downtime and the necessary study time. I trust you! Let's see what you come up with." Say to your toddler, "You have great ideas. How can you make sure nobody slips on your corn?"

TRY THIS STRATEGY INSTEAD

If your toddler shrugs or says she doesn't have any ideas, you can prompt her with, "What about pushing it to the side of your plate instead of dropping it on the floor?" Then follow up with, "What else can you do?" If your pre-teen doesn't seem to be interested in engaging with you, you may have to encourage cooperation with a logical consequence. Say, "I see you don't want to talk about it. When you are ready to brainstorm, I'm here. Until then, I'll hold on to the TV remote."

Lack of Self-Reflection

Self-reflection is a fundamental skill that leads to self-awareness. A person who can reflect on his own thought patterns, speech habits, and actions is a step closer to managing difficult impulses and emotions. Self-reflection also strengthens our interpersonal relationships because it can improve the quality of our interactions with those around us.

For children at all developmental stages, self-reflection is a challenge because it's a skill that develops over time as they mature. Young children lack this skill because by nature they tend to live in the present. They are also process-oriented, which means their primary desire is to learn through discovery. As mentioned in step 2, young children lack an inner dialogue to help them interpret the past.

Without this ability to consider past circumstances, it's difficult for children to look inward, analyze their choices, and reflect on how they can improve. As children mature, they start to understand that it's important to try to be better. They learn this when practicing sports or studying for tests.

GUIDED SELF-REFLECTION

It's a big leap for children to go from improving their test scores to reflecting on how they can improve their character overall. Let's consider a few scenarios to figure out how you can help bridge the gap.

Your teenager got into a fight with his friend because he didn't save a spot in the line to buy baseball tickets. His friend wasn't able to go to the game and is now angry. Your teen refuses to acknowledge any wrongdoing.

Your kindergartener gets annoyed with his sister for using his video games and calls her stupid. He is unapologetic when she gets upset.

Reflect together: Ask your teen, "Why do you think your friend is angry with you?" Allow your teen to express himself, even if he doesn't assume responsibility. Ask your kindergartener, "Why is your sister sad?"

Brainstorm alternatives: Challenge your child to come up with different ways he could have handled the situation. Even if he maintains he did nothing wrong, say, "I understand you are standing by your behavior. But we can always improve and do better. What could you have done or said differently?"

Develop good habits: Encourage activities conducive to deeper introspection. For a teen, suggest a daily journal. For a kindergartener, it could take the form of an art project like drawing or painting, with appropriate prompts from you. For example, "Can you draw a picture showing how you felt when your sister used your video games?"

The skill of self-reflection is important in the self-growth journey. Self-reflection is important for you, too. You can model this skill to your children through journaling or other healthy outlets, like music or art.

Modeling Emotional Management

The ability to handle positive and negative emotions is crucial to living a productive and healthy life. One of our responsibilities is to demonstrate healthy emotional regulation so our children can learn from our example.

Sensitivity to Criticism

Children of all ages, especially those approaching or experiencing puberty, are prone to feeling defensive or sensitive to criticism. Whether they're being scolded, corrected, or disagreed with, a child who is sensitive to criticism may get angry and lash out or could become sad and withdraw.

If you handle this type of sensitivity appropriately, you can usually keep it at bay. Sensitivity to criticism can be beneficial if it motivates children to better themselves. It becomes destructive only when it snowballs into anxiety or overwhelming feelings of sadness or anger.

It's important to distinguish between a highly sensitive child and a typical child who can be sensitive from time to time. A highly sensitive child, as defined by Dr. Elaine Aron, refers to "one of the 15 to 20 percent of children born with a nervous system that is highly aware and quick to react to everything." This physiological condition leaves a child vulnerable to everyday interactions with others. Highly sensitive children also tend to be sensory-seeking or sensory-avoiding, similar to those who have challenges with sensory integration, as mentioned in step 3.

RESPONDING TO A SENSITIVE CHILD

Consider the following situations:

Your teen comes home from school sobbing and says her drama teacher said she needs to work harder at memorizing her lines.

Your toddler breaks down in tears when you scold her for drawing on the wall.

Whether you have a highly sensitive child or a child who experiences moments of heightened sensitivity, the following techniques can help.

First, connect: A sensitive child is usually at her most vulnerable immediately following the upsetting incident. Before you even start the conversation or give any input, invite your child to sit next to you or on your lap. If she is receptive, hold her hand or put your hand on her back. Physical touch communicates to your child that no matter what, you care about her and are on her side.

Validate: Identify the emotions your child is feeling. Say to your teen, "I totally understand why you're so upset. Did you feel disappointed because you've been working so hard and she didn't see it?" Allow your teen to express herself without interjection or judgment, even if it seems like an overreaction. Say to your toddler, "I see you're so sad after I told you not to draw on the wall."

Evaluate the situation: Once you've validated their emotions, approach the facts of the situation. Remember, when children are sensitive, they spend a significant amount of time berating themselves, so be sure not to add extra toughness to the situation. Say to your teen, "What do you think about what your teacher told you about memorizing your lines?" Then follow up with, "Do you think any part of her criticism is accurate?" Say to your toddler, "What do you think about drawing on the walls?"

When you open up the situation for discussion without giving any opinions, your child will be more likely to view it objectively. It's vital that you invite your child to think without giving any type of direction or judgment.

AVOID THIS
Avoid giving consequences for your child's outbursts or original infraction, like drawing on the wall. Children who are sensitive to criticism have punished themselves enough through their emotional reactions to that criticism. Sensitivity to criticism can send them into a spiral of shame. Giving them consequences may deepen their shame and guilt instead of helping them grow from this experience. Discussing it with you is sufficient in painting a clearer and more objective picture for them.

Pessimism and Low Confidence
Although most children, especially young ones, are generally content, some get stuck in stretches of negative thinking. Occasionally this can be a result of mood disorders like anxiety or depression, but for most children, pessimism is a defense mechanism. For example, if children experience a negative interaction, they may be wary when approaching a similar situation. Or, just like adults,

some children may be naturally more prone to negative thinking than others.

If a child takes his pessimism to heart, he may have less motivation to engage in everyday tasks or fulfill responsibilities. This can lead to self-defeat or apathy. In general, pessimistic outlooks and behaviors are most common in school-age children and teenagers.

MODELING A GROWTH MINDSET

A growth mindset refers to the belief system that each person has the ability to grow, develop, and improve. Adopting this mindset is essential for parenting success, and you must also model it for and teach it to your children. We often see a growth mindset in contrast to its opposite, a fixed mindset, which is a belief system rooted in the idea that our talents and intelligence are unchanging.

Parents can teach a growth mindset by constantly communicating that our children are in control of their abilities and the outcomes of their choices and supporting their drive to learn, practice, and be better people. A growth mindset is a cornerstone of our goal as conscious parents, as we are on a journey of growth and can teach our children to do the same. Being better today than yesterday is the foundation of a growth mindset and leads to success.

HANDLING PESSIMISM

Your school-age child has a soccer game tomorrow and you find her lounging around instead of practicing like her coach instructed. You ask why she's not practicing, and she says, "Eh, I know we're going to lose anyway, so what's the point?"

Be curious: Ask your child, "What's the worst thing that could happen if you actually practice like your coach asked you to?" Be prepared for a fresh retort and respond with a smile. Then continue with your questioning until she answers seriously.

Challenge assumptions: Gently confront your child's negative thinking: "How do you know that it'll turn out that way? Can you be sure?" If your child responds affirmatively, feel free to respond lightly and humorously. You can even say something like, "Do you have a crystal ball somewhere that you're not telling me about?" Communicate that there's no possible way she can predict the future.

Compliment your child's abilities: Say, "I know you're a talented soccer player because I've seen you play. Imagine how much better you could be if you practice."

Remind your child about her responsibilities: At the very least, she has a responsibility to her soccer team to be the best she can be on the field, even if the outcome won't be favorable.

BOOSTING CONFIDENCE

Children may experience low confidence for a variety of reasons. As parents, we have an obligation to explore our children's experiences and ascertain whether our children are chronically low on self-confidence or the feeling comes and goes. The former may require more work. Children who constantly feel bad about themselves could be experiencing underlying feelings of inadequacy stemming from negative experiences such as bullying, lack of connection to family or friends, or depression.

When our children are still young, we get a front-row seat to the majority of their experiences. But as they grow and become more independent, they spend less time with us and more time interacting with the world. We can only discover what our children are truly going through by communicating with them.

Consider the following examples.

Your teenager has a tough time making friends because he's too anxious to join any clubs.

Your school-age child has a hard time choosing even the simplest things. You ask him what color ice pop he wants, and he waits for other children to answer before he repeats what they say.

Verbalize needs: Coach your child to have confidence in his needs and desires. Give him the words to express himself if his anxiety is impeding his ability to access them.

Assign jobs: Every week, give your child a different job to complete at home. Be sure to choose tasks that contribute to the overall cohesiveness of the way your home runs.

Acknowledge the effort: Don't gush. Children can feel when you're being insincere.

Celebrate the positive contributions: Every little acknowledgment strengthens your child's confidence a little bit, even if what he accomplished seems petty or insignificant. Say it out loud: "Wow! It was so helpful when you put your laundry in the hamper. Now I won't have to pick it up!" or "You gave your sister a turn with the toy! Way to go!"

Teaching Cognitive Flexibility

As discussed in step 2, cognitive flexibility is one of the main executive functioning skills. In the next two sections, you'll get concrete techniques and dialogue examples to help your children develop cognitive flexibility.

When fully developed in children, flexible thinking sets a foundation for a lifetime of learning and growing. Flexibility helps children see situations and conflicts from various perspectives. This allows them to come up with different ways to tackle challenges and to see a problem through other people's eyes. This ability is extremely beneficial, as it leads to increased empathy and compassion, as well as stronger problem-solving skills.

Children who have a tough time with flexible thinking may also suffer academically because rigid thinking won't help them analyze nuances of meaning in a reading passage or come up with creative solutions to a math problem. Helping children develop this skill is extremely important.

Inflexibility

Your school-age child gets angry and stops playing a game of tag at a friend's birthday party because the other kids are following an unfamiliar set of rules.

Your toddler has a tantrum in the morning because he wants to keep building with magnetic tiles instead of going to school.

Establish the facts: Ask your school-age child, "What happened at the birthday party that made you angry?" Say to your toddler, "You are so upset because I asked you to clean up your toys."

Validate emotions: Acknowledge and name your child's feelings. Say to your school-age child, "I can imagine it's frustrating to have to learn new rules to a game you already know." (Note: It's possible your child felt left out or socially embarrassed because he didn't know something everyone else knew. You can address that by adding, "I know it can be embarrassing when you feel left out. It's okay not to know the new rules.") Say to your toddler, "I can tell you're frustrated because you were having so much fun building your tower."

Change the rules: Choose another game to play with your school-age child. Change the rules and explore how much fun you can have. For example, say, "Let's play Uno. But instead of matching colors, let's do the opposite and only put down a card if it's a different color." Your child may be hesitant at first, but he'll soon see that it can be fun to do things differently.

Teach: Explain that if he had tried to play the new game of tag, he might have had fun. But by refusing to play, he was guaranteed to have a miserable time.

Give timed warnings: When taking out the magnetic tiles in the morning, look your toddler in the eye and tell him he is playing for only 10 minutes and then it's time to clean up and go to school. Two minutes before cleanup time, approach your toddler, make eye contact, and remind him that he has two minutes left to play.

Children of all ages have a hard time with transitions. Rigid thinkers need time to process the routine presented to them. A concrete timed warning will help your child be more comfortable transitioning than being told abruptly that he needs to stop. Sand timers are a great tool to give young children a concrete understanding of time.

Perfectionism

Children who have a high drive to succeed usually hold themselves to a high standard. Children who are prone to perfectionism, however, constantly feel disappointed in themselves. Before we focus on handling perfectionism in children, let's distinguish between perfectionism and a healthy desire to succeed.

PERFECTIONISM	DRIVE TO SUCCEED
Unrealistic goals	Self-imposed high standards
Constantly disappointed in achievements	Generally satisfied with results
Results in self-deprecation	Results in high energy and a desire to continue succeeding
Leads to feelings of inadequacy	Boosts self-esteem

As you can see, there's a stark difference between a healthy drive to succeed (which should be celebrated) and the self-imposed unhealthy and unrealistic pressure of perfectionism. Here's how to coach kids to let go of perfectionism:

Your teenager seems nervous in the morning and tells you that he's getting his math midterm back today. When he comes home from school, he snaps at you at every turn. When you ask how he did on the math test, he tells you that he got 10 points lower than he had hoped, although he still got an A.

Here's an in-the-moment technique to help your child work through a specific episode of perfectionism and the difficult emotions that typically follow.

Support and encourage: Say to your teen, "You worked so hard. You are valuable no matter what." Although this seems obvious and maybe even unnecessary, it's important to convey unconditional support. Teenagers especially may scoff at your demonstrations of affection, but they still have a deep craving for that support.

Validate feelings: Even if it seems silly that he is disappointed about an A, push aside those feelings of judgment. Say, "It must be disappointing not to perform as well as you had hoped."

Set realistic goals: Remind your child nobody is perfect. Explain that perfection is unattainable. Cite examples of real people who succeeded in life despite mistakes and obstacles. Albert Einstein, Bill Gates, J. K. Rowling, and Mark Zuckerberg are just a few examples.

Reassure your child: Make sure he knows that even when he doesn't do as well as he'd hoped, or even if he failed the test completely, he's still loved and appreciated.

Check assumptions: Challenge his belief that he is a failure if he doesn't live up to his own high expectations. Say, "Not being perfect doesn't make you a failure. It makes you human. Let's come up with some realistic goals together."

Easily Frustrated

Children who experience bouts of anxiety or set unrealistic goals can become easily frustrated. Sometimes children who have a hard time regulating emotions become overwhelmed by their own feelings of frustration. Children can also become easily frustrated when they face an obstacle beyond their control that prevents them from getting what they want, whether it's a relationship, an item, or a particular outcome.

As children mature and begin to understand their emotions more deeply, they start to develop the coping skills necessary to handle frustration without reacting in a destructive way. A child who has a mature understanding of frustration may pause, understand she is feeling frustrated, take a deep breath, and busy herself with another task before returning to the first one.

COPING WITH FRUSTRATION

You can teach kids healthy ways to cope with frustration in any situation. Here are some tips:

Your teenager screams at you and stomps her feet because you told her you can't drive her to her friend's house.

Your preschooler throws a toy because it's not working the way she wants it to.

Validate feelings: Acknowledge and name your child's feelings. Say to your teenager, "I can imagine it's frustrating to not be able to do the things you want to do." Say to your preschooler, "It's frustrating when your toys don't work the way you want them to." Naming frustration helps your child begin to recognize when she is feeling that way and communicates understanding and empathy.

Breathe mindfully: Encourage the breathing techniques you have taught your children on calm occasions.

Set limits: Although it's normal for children to feel frustrated, your child needs to understand there are unacceptable ways to communicate it. Say to your teenager, "I know you're frustrated. Everyone feels that way sometimes. But you may not scream at me." Say to your preschooler, "I know you're frustrated, but throwing a toy can hurt someone."

Brainstorm alternatives: Say to your teenager, "It's important to find a healthy way to express your frustration so you can work through and get past it. What are some more respectful ways to express that you're frustrated?" As she comes up with ideas, respond encouragingly and positively. Ask your preschooler, "What's a safer way to tell me you're frustrated?" Don't allow for an easy way out. Make sure your child comes up with a few ideas.

TRY THIS STRATEGY INSTEAD

If your child has difficulty accessing the proper words, give her some suggestions. Say, "Maybe you can take a deep breath and say, 'Mommy, this isn't working. Can you help me?'"

Fear of Change

Fear of change is a common experience for children who lack strong executive functioning skills. This fear may stem from an underlying insecurity, like past trauma. Children who have experienced trauma may be less resilient to uncertainty and change.

In a study by Dr. Christine Courtois, children who experience trauma as the result of child abuse or war have a harder time adjusting to new routines or change in their environments. Some children feel fearful because they lack positive human connection. Others are going through too many changes at once. Many children, especially toddlers, simply haven't developmentally reached a state that allows them to adapt to changes in routine, surroundings, or circumstances.

Your family moved to a different city, and your pre-teen is acting out. His usually easygoing personality has become volatile and irritable. You ask him to take the garbage out and he snaps at you.

Since the move, your toddler cries easily and has a hard time calming down.

Validate feelings: Set aside some time when you can sit with your child one-on-one. Say to your pre-teen, "I know there have been a lot of changes in your life lately." Just acknowledging this fact can provide a huge feeling of relief for your child.

A toddler might not be able to understand or recognize this deeper fear or change, so you might say, "This feels new and scary. I understand. I love you no matter what."

Develop a game plan together: Propose the idea to your pre-teen that you would like to sit together every day after school and talk about the day. Giving your child this outlet can help him feel supported during this time of change.

Setting and Achieving Goals

The ability to set and achieve goals also falls under the executive functioning skill set. It can take a lifetime to master. Sharpening this skill can reap many benefits, like boosting your child's motivation to succeed and fostering an optimistic attitude.

Poor Organization

When children exhibit poor organization, people often assume they are lazy or messy, but that isn't necessarily the case. Young children may have a problem with organization because that part of their executive functioning isn't fully developed yet. Many will become more organized as they get older.

Other children develop this skill more slowly than their peers, which can be frustrating for everyone. Some experience moments of disorganization because of stress or fatigue, which can slow the performance of the prefrontal cortex. Let's discuss how you can help improve organization skills in your kids.

Your school-age child has a science fair coming up. He spends all his time doing other activities he enjoys and seems to ignore your constant reminders to work on his display. A day before the science fair, he throws together a project that looks sloppy, and he gets a poor grade.

Your preschooler takes a long time getting ready in the morning. You are constantly asking him to put on his shoes. Five minutes before it's time to leave, you ask him where his shoes are, and he tells you he can't find them.

Reassure your child: Tell him you know he's not lazy or messy. Name some specific strengths he possesses.

Show support: State that you know he wants to be organized and you're here to help him figure out a better system.

Create tools: Offer to help your school-age child create his own planner, checklist, schedule, or whiteboard. Work together with your preschooler on a visual schedule.

For most children, any tactile and concrete organizational tools can be extremely helpful. But not every tool is helpful in the same way. Ask for your child's input on what works best for him. If you include him in the process, he'll be more likely to use it.

Indecisiveness

The inability to make decisions can be the result of a lack of judgment. Until the judgment center of the brain is fully developed, children and even teenagers may not be capable of thinking through hypothetical scenarios or the long-term consequences of their decisions. They may not be able to make a decision at all, or they might make the wrong one. Older children may exhibit indecisiveness because they understand that if they choose one option, they'll lose an equally attractive one.

Your teenager needs to choose which college to go to. The deadline is drawing near, and you're worried she's going to be left with no options.

You and your toddler are in an ice cream parlor and there's a line forming behind you. She's having a tough time deciding and doesn't care about the crowd of people waiting.

Validate feelings: Say to your teenager, "I know this is a tough decision to make." Say to your toddler, "You must love ice cream so much that you're having a hard time choosing a flavor."

Remember you're in it together: Assure your teenager you'll support any choice she makes. Gently emphasize that she must decide on a school by a certain time. Tell her, "Let's sit down together and come up with a list of pros and cons. Then you can take a day to think about it."

Offer choices: Give your toddler two choices. Tell her, "You can choose cherry or chocolate. I'll set a timer on my phone for one minute. If you don't choose by then, I can choose for you."

Explain potential consequences: Remind your teenager that colleges take deadlines seriously. If she doesn't give you an answer by tomorrow, she could lose her spot and be stuck with nowhere to go. All her friends will be going off to college, and she will have to figure out what to do instead. Show your toddler the line growing behind you so she can see that other people are waiting.

Lack of Follow-Through

Taking responsibility and being accountable are not innate skills. They have to be taught and reinforced.

When our children are young, we forgive their constant shift of attention from one activity to another. If a child is finished kicking a ball, we don't get upset when he suddenly stops and starts pursuing something else. When they grow into adolescence and the subsequent teenage years, we start to expect more. As their capacity for responsibility grows, so do our expectations.

Teenagers get excited quickly. A study by Sally Brown and Kate Guthrie showed that many high-risk behaviors in teenagers are the result of their capacity to "be in the moment." They can be incredibly passionate and committed about something until something else grabs their attention. This shift in interest isn't meant to drive us crazy, but to allow them to continuously explore their newly acquired independence.

Your teen has been slacking on his chore of setting the table for dinner. He also told you he wants to quit the baseball team. He now wants to go to the skate park after school.

Celebrate past success: Identify a time when he did follow through on his promise, even if it was minor. Talk about how great that was and how accomplished he felt.

Discuss why: Explain that everyone has responsibilities. If we don't uphold ours, the cohesive family unit can fall apart. Give the metaphor of a sports team. If one position isn't covered, the other team will score.

Noticing Attempts to Rescue

As parents, our primary desire is to take away our children's discomfort and pain. When you find yourself tempted to pluck your child out of uncomfortable or painful situations, remember that rescuing them will not teach them the necessary life skills to tackle similar situations head-on. It actually accomplishes the opposite because they will learn to be dependent on you to save them when the going gets tough.

When you feel overwhelmed by handling the pain of seeing your children suffer when you let them make mistakes, remember you won't be around in every situation to save them. Allowing them to learn from their mistakes ensures they'll have the skills to handle adversity in the future.

It's hard to see our children struggle, but being there to support them, encourage them, and teach them the skills to conquer challenges will be worth it in the end. Our role as parents is to be their teacher and coach, not their savior.

Enforce accountability: Use logical consequences. Tell your teen, "If you can't set the table for dinner, then you can't enjoy the privilege of watching TV." You can also tell him that if he's not going to fulfill his commitment to the baseball team and his coach, he'll have to come straight home after school.

Learning Differences

Other factors can contribute to poor executive functioning. If your child's development is particularly delayed, or if the techniques in the book aren't working, you may want to consult a professional diagnostician to rule out the following learning or thinking differences in your children:

Attention deficit hyperactivity disorder (ADHD) is a learning disability that affects executive functioning. Children with ADHD may show impulsivity, inattentiveness, hyperfocus, and challenges with organization, planning, time management, and emotional regulation.

Dyslexia is a neurological learning disorder characterized by difficulty reading. Because children with dyslexia spend so much time and mental energy trying to make sense of written words, they may become distracted, disruptive, oppositional, or frustrated.

Auditory processing disorder (APD) affects the ability to understand and process speech. Children with APD have a hard time paying attention because they don't understand what they're hearing and easily lose focus. They may also withdraw in noisy environments.

Sensory processing disorder (SPD) is covered in step 3.

If you think your child could be experiencing any of these challenges, seek professional advice from your pediatrician for a proper diagnosis. Early intervention and academic and sensory accommodations can help many exceptional children thrive.

Resolving Conflict

It's easy to fall into unproductive communication styles when you're handling conflict with your children. Here are some ways to combat these ineffective and counterproductive types of conflict resolution.

Bargaining

Constant negotiations with your children can be exhausting. When given an expectation or limitation, many strong-willed children would rather argue and barter than go down without a fight. Desire for autonomy is a driving force behind this behavior. But how do we nip it in the bud so it doesn't result in a dragged-out argument or worse?

> *Your teenager asks if she can go to the movies with her friends. You tell her she can't because she has too much homework. She tries to negotiate by bartering the right to go to the movies with future chores around the house.*

> *Your kindergartener asks for a toy while you're shopping at Target and you tell her no. She asks again and you say no. She continues to bargain by saying, "Come on, Daddy. I'll clean up all my toys at home if you get me the toy."*

The following technique is presented by Lynn Lott, a positive discipline expert, and can work for any age:

Ask: "Have you ever heard of the game 'Asked and Answered'?" (Your child will say no.)

Restate: Ask your teen, "Did you ask me about going to the movies?" Ask your kindergartener, "Did you ask me for a toy?" Your child will say yes.

Set limits: "Did I give you an answer?" Your child will probably say yes and resume bargaining. Say, "I already answered you and my answer was no. Please do not ask me again, because the answer will not change."

Each subsequent attempt to bargain with you should be met with a single response: "Asked and answered."

Expecting Rewards

Most of the world runs on a system of reward and punishment. Even if you don't use this system in your home, your child is learning at school, on sports teams, and in his general life experience that if he does something positive, he'll be rewarded. Children learn quickly that this is an effective way to get nice things from you.

You ask your school-age child to get his dirty laundry off the floor. When he completes the task, he approaches you and says, "I picked it up. Can I have a Popsicle now?"

Your teenager comes home with an improved grade on his test. He gives it to you and says, "Now will you get me that new video game?"

To break the habit of expecting rewards, offer to replace a material reward with an opportunity to connect. Say to your school-age child, "You picked up your clothes like I asked you to. Great! Now that the floor is clean, we can play Monopoly like you asked me to the other day." Say to your teenager, "It's amazing that you improved so much since last time! Let's celebrate by watching that movie you were waiting to see."

Try This Strategy Instead

If you're looking for other ways to engage and assess your child's behavior, try the following.

Positive Affirmations

Many of the behaviors discussed in this chapter have a basis in poor executive functioning skills, which can easily lead to low self-esteem. Positive affirmations are an effective way to strengthen your children's sense of self.

Sit with your child during a moment of calm and brainstorm a list of positive self-talk statements together. Create a visual cue and hang it on the wall as a reminder to use these affirmations daily. Examples include "I'm going to do my best today!" and "I am enough."

Gratitude Journals

Another way to help your child stay positive and develop a growth mindset is to teach him to be grateful for all the blessings and positivity in his life.

Go to the store together and let him pick out a journal. Challenge him to write in his journal daily, answering various prompts that inspire gratitude. Here are some examples:

"What is your favorite thing that happened this week?"

"What do you want to accomplish today?"

"Name something you do very well."

You can also find journals that include writing prompts targeting different age groups and interests.

MANTRAS

I'm here to help you learn the tools you need. We are in this together.

When I feel the desire to rescue my child, I resist. She is learning and growing.

I will guide you to become aware of your strengths and weaknesses.

RECAP

- ▶ Emotional self-regulation occurs on a learning curve.

- ▶ When children are young, we act as their constant guardians to keep them safe. As they get older, our role should shift into that of a coach or facilitator.

- ▶ Most children live in the now and are process-oriented. This leads to a general lack of self-reflection.

- ▶ Emotional management is crucial in leading a productive life.

- ▶ Cognitive flexibility allows children to shift their mindsets and see situations from other perspectives.

- ▶ Unlike a healthy drive to succeed, perfectionism is driven by unrealistic goals that lead to feelings of inadequacy.

▶ What insights have you gained about guiding your child to find solutions to their own problems?

▶ Which of these challenging behaviors resonates with you most?

▶ How do you feel about implementing some of these strategies to improve your child's executive functioning skills?

STAY CONNECTED

You did it! Congratulations on going outside your comfort zone with the desire and willingness to question, assess, and improve your parenting methods. So far, you have learned about various mistaken behaviors, their possible causes, and in-the-moment techniques to help you transform moments of conflict into opportunities for growth and connection. But the hard work doesn't end here. Conscious parenting is a continuous journey of discovery and growth for you and your children. This chapter explores how to foster and maintain a culture of conscious parenting at home using ongoing mindful practices and rituals for your entire family.

Cultivating Mindfulness

As we've discovered, achieving emotional regulation is the most important aspect of approaching conflict with consciousness. Here are some ongoing self-regulation exercises that, if practiced regularly, can help you maintain a deep level of mindfulness and help you through those moments of chaos.

Body Scan
The body scan can help you feel relatively calm and relaxed throughout your busy day. You can do it lying down or sitting still.

Close your eyes: Focus on your breathing, becoming aware of its rhythm.

Focus on your body: How does it feel? Cold? Warm? Concentrate on the fabric of your clothing and how it feels against your skin.

Slowly scan your body: Spend a few seconds concentrating on each area of your body, from your toes to your head. Linger on each part. Do you have any aches? Are you relaxed, or are your muscles pulling tightly?

Open your eyes: Once you have scanned your entire body, open your eyes.

You can do this mindfulness exercise at any time, but I recommend at least once when you wake up in the morning and are still lying in bed, as well as in the car when you are about to see your children at the end of the day.

Mindful "Seeing"

Sometimes our preconceived thoughts can become stifling. Here's an exercise to help break through the clutter in your mind. Find a seat near a window.

Sit still: Focus on every object you can see.

See: Notice traits, colors, textures, and sounds, instead of labeling them as trees, animals, clouds, and so on.

Observe: Do these objects move or remain still? Try to focus on the concept that this is just a tiny snapshot of the greater world. Ask yourself, "How would someone who has never seen this scene view it?"

This mindfulness exercise is essential in maintaining calm in the heat of the moment. The more often you do it, the stronger your ability to pause and regain composure.

Five Senses Exercise

You can practice this exercise in any situation, scenario, or environment to bring yourself to a state of mindfulness when you're short on time. While seated in a comfortable spot, look around and notice things you can feel with your five senses:

Find one thing you can see: Notice all its details: its colors, patterns, and size. Name an attribute you wouldn't normally notice.

Find one thing you can feel: Is it smooth? Bumpy? Cold? Warm? This can be your clothing, something in your surroundings, or anything else that is easily accessible.

Find one thing you can hear: Determine where the sound is coming from. Is it in the foreground or the background? Is it loud? Is it sudden or constant?

Find one thing you can smell: Close your eyes and focus on a scent that you may or may not usually filter out. Is it pleasant? Is it unpleasant? Does it smell like it belongs in your immediate environment, or is it intrusive?

Find one thing you can taste: If you're eating, drinking, or chewing something, focus on that. If not, how does your mouth taste right now? You can even open your mouth and survey the air around you.

This is particularly helpful when you start to feel stress or anxiety, or during fast-paced situations, such as getting your children ready in the morning or ready for bed at night.

Creating Routines

Children of all ages thrive on regular routines. Not only do these rituals create and foster a sense of security and safety for your child, but they also allow you to connect on a consistent basis. I can't stress enough the importance of these steady and continual opportunities for connection.

Family Cheer

Mornings can be one of the most chaotic times of the day. Juggling work and school preparations, cooking breakfast, getting dressed, and making sure your kids get to school on time can be extremely stressful.

As a result, we often start our day in a state of disconnect. Children are sent to school or day care feeling insecure and can be prone to misbehaviors and conflict. Implementing a family cheer allows your family unit the opportunity to reconnect before everyone goes their separate ways.

The best part of this ritual is that it's so simple to create and practice. Huddle like a sports team, throw your hands in the middle, and shout, "Smith family!" or something else that reflects your family's values. This will be your children's last memory before school, rather than the moments of mayhem leading up to it.

Dance Parties

We learned in step 1 about the benefits of music for the brain, as it elicits an instant release of the happy hormones dopamine and serotonin. These chemicals create a feeling of calm and peacefulness and set up the brain to be more receptive to learning and listening.

Like music, dancing also leads to a release of oxytocin and natural opioids in the brain. Combining music and dancing can improve feelings of connection right away.

In moments of stress or in times of harmony, putting on some music and dancing with your children creates an atmosphere of love and collaboration.

Safe Spaces

When implemented appropriately, safe spaces provide the opportunity for children to self-regulate on their own time. A safe space should be a designated area in your home. It should be comfortable and cozy (think pillows, blankets, stuffed animals) and have tools such as books and sensory bottles to assist your child in self-regulation.

Remember, safe spaces should never be used as a time-out, but as a place of respite for your child to retreat to in moments of chaos or conflict. You can read more about how to use safe spaces in steps 3 and 4.

In times of calm, show your child the safe space. Ask her to contribute to the setup and what you keep there. If your child understands the purpose of the safe space, she will be more likely to take refuge there when she needs to.

Visual Schedules

Children of all ages respond well to images. Young children connect to images especially deeply because of their inability to read words. Sit with your child and brainstorm different tasks and responsibilities to include in a visual schedule.

The benefits of these schedules are immense. Children have so much to remember that they can be overwhelmed and have difficulty managing their responsibilities. This stress can lead to all types of negative behavior.

If children participate in creating the schedule, they will be more likely to want to follow it. Make it fun—let them decorate and get as creative as they want!

Deep Breathing Exercises

This book stresses the physiological importance of deep belly breathing and the calming effect it has on all of us, parents and children alike. To help your child with emotional regulation, reinforce these conscious techniques during calm, peaceful moments so when stressful situations arise, he can access them easily.

Tell your child to place his hand on his stomach.

Ask him what parts of his body move when he breathes.

Instruct him to breathe deeply and slowly so his belly, not his shoulders, moves in and out. This will take some practice.

Once he has mastered this diaphragmatic breathing, slowly guide him through exhalation and inhalation. Practice daily.

Breathing through a straw can also help your child achieve this type of breathing. Blowing bubbles through a bubble wand trains your child to breathe in a slow and even way.

Building Relationships

Human connection is so important to a child's healthy development. Although parents and primary caregivers play the most important role in a child's development, siblings, community, teachers, and friends are also integral in contributing to your child's success. It truly does take a village to raise a child.

Here are routines that can help foster a greater sense of belonging for your children.

Family Meetings

When we're navigating the hustle and bustle of daily life, it's easy to forget to check in as a family. As adults, we may be able to cope without this check-in, but our children need the connection.

One way to ensure all the members of your family are feeling represented, seen, and validated is to schedule regular family meetings. Ideally, these meetings would occur daily at the dinner table when everyone is present. If that does not seem feasible, make sure to check in at least once a week.

My family sits together every Saturday. Each person has the floor, uninterrupted, to talk about his or her challenges and accomplishments for the week. We refer to these as our "grows" and "glows."

Community Involvement

Getting involved in the greater community is key in raising conscientious and empathetic children who have compassion for others. Create opportunities for your children to practice giving to others.

Find a community center in your area and inquire about volunteer opportunities you can do as a family, such as preparing meals at a soup kitchen or packing up or delivering supplies to those in need. Your children will begin to feel the positive effects of connecting to the greater community around them.

Pen Pal Systems

This old-fashioned communication is hugely beneficial for children once they can read and write. Establishing a meaningful connection with a child from a different place, who experiences different circumstances, can help develop your child's cognitive flexibility, an executive functioning skill that is strengthened when a child is able to understand another person's perspective.

Corresponding with a pen pal also teaches patience, compassion, and social skills like reciprocation. Feeling connected encourages positive behavior, and the excitement that comes from receiving a letter can also foster true happiness.

For a more modern take on traditional pen pals, you can also sign up for email pen pals. Various organizations online match up children for this purpose.

- ▶ You can practice mindfulness in any circumstance or location.
- ▶ Children of all ages and developmental stages thrive on rituals and routines.
- ▶ Dancing triggers the release of oxytocin and natural opioids in the brain.
- ▶ Safe spaces shouldn't be used to avoid responsibilities, but for practicing mindfulness, introspection, and emotional regulation.
- ▶ Cultivating relationships is imperative in maintaining healthy connections in our children's lives.

REFLECT

- ▶ Do you have any rituals you're already practicing as a family?
- ▶ Which exercise offered here feels most practical for you?
- ▶ Which routine or ritual are you most excited to begin implementing in your home?

RESOURCES

Books

The Conscious Parent: Transforming Ourselves, Empowering Our Children by Dr. Shefali Tsabary

How to Talk So Kids Will Listen and Listen So Kids Will Talk by Adele Faber and Elaine Mazlish

No Bad Kids: Toddler Discipline Without Shame by Janet Lansbury

Parenting from the Inside Out: How a Deeper Self-Understanding Can Help You Raise Children Who Thrive by Daniel J. Siegel and Mary Hartzell

Peaceful Parent, Happy Kids: How to Stop Yelling and Start Connecting by Dr. Laura Markham

Positive Discipline: The Classic Guide to Helping Children Develop Self-Discipline, Responsibility, Cooperation, and Problem-Solving Skills by Jane Nelsen, Ed.D.

Raising Your Spirited Child: A Guide for Parents Whose Child Is More Intense, Sensitive, Perceptive, Persistent, and Energetic by Mary Sheedy Kurcinka

The Whole-Brain Child: 12 Revolutionary Strategies to Nurture Your Child's Developing Mind by Daniel J. Siegel and Tina Payne Bryson

Podcast

Respectful Parenting: Janet Lansbury Unruffled

REFERENCES

Ackerman, Courtney E. "22 Mindfulness Exercises, Techniques, and Activities for Adults." *PositivePsychology.com*. Accessed April 2020. positivepsychology.com /mindfulness-exercises-techniques-activities/.

Aron, Elaine N. *The Highly Sensitive Child: Helping Our Children Thrive When the World Overwhelms Them.* New York: Harmony Books, 2002.

Bannan, Karen J. "Why Toddlers Always Say 'No!'" *Parents.com*. Accessed March 2020. parents.com/toddlers -preschoolers/development/behavioral/why-toddlers -always-say-no/.

BMJ. "What's on Your Surgeon's Playlist?" *EurekaAlert!*. December 11, 2014. eurekalert.org/pub_releases/2014-12 /bmj-woy121014.php.

Bowen, Will. *Complaint Free Relationships: Transforming Your Life One Relationship at a Time.* New York: Harmony Books, 2009.

Brown, Sally, and Kate Guthrie. "Why Don't Teenagers Use Contraception? A Qualitative Interview Study." *European Journal of Contraception and Reproductive Health Care* 15, no. 3 (2010): 197–204. doi.org/10.3109 /13625181003763456.

Center for Parenting Education. "Perfectionism in Children." Accessed April 2020. centerforparenting

education.org/library-of-articles/school-and
-learning-issues/perfectionism-in-children/.

Center on the Developing Child at Harvard University.
"Brain Architecture." Accessed March 2020.
developingchild.harvard.edu/science/key-concepts
/brain-architecture/.

———. "Executive Function and Self-Regulation." Accessed
March 2020. developingchild.harvard.edu/science
/key-concepts/executive-function/.

Chang, Rosemarie Sokol, and Nicholas S. Thompson. "The
Attention-Getting Capacity of Whines and Child-
Directed Speech." *Evolutionary Psychology* 8, no. 2 (2010).
doi.org/10.1177/147470491000800209.

Cleveland Clinic. "What Happens to Your Body During the
Fight or Flight Response?" December 9, 2019. health
.clevelandclinic.org/what-happens-to-your-body-during
-the-fight-or-flight-response/.

Courtois, Christine A. "Complex Trauma, Complex Reactions: Assessment and Treatment." *Psychotherapy: Theory,
Research, Practice, Training* 41, no. 4 (2004): 412–25.
doi.org/10.1037/0033-3204.41.4.412.

Crisis Text Line. "How to Deal with Self Harm." Accessed
April 2020. crisistextline.org/topics/self-harm/#types
-of-self-harm-2.

Davis, Jeanie Lerche. "Teenagers: Why Do They Rebel?"
WebMD. Accessed March 2020. webmd.com
/parenting/features/teenagers-why-do-they-rebel#1.

Diproperzio, Linda. "Language Development Milestones: Ages 1 to 4." *Parents.com.* Accessed March 2020. parents .com/toddlers-preschoolers/development/language /language-development-milestones-ages-1-to-4/.

Franz, Julia. "Teenage Indecision? That's Just the Growing Brain, a New Study Says." *The World.* January 29, 2017. pri.org/stories/2017-01-29/teenage-indecision-s-just -growing-brain-new-study-says.

Fraser-Thill, Rebecca. "Benefits of Having a Pen Pal." *VeryWell Family.* October 22, 2019. verywellfamily .com/benefits-of-having-a-pen-pal-3288504.

Gartrell, Dan. *A Guidance Approach for the Encouraging Classroom.* Belmont, CA: Wadsworth Cengage, 2014.

Gathercole, Susan. E. "The Development of Memory." *Journal of Child Psychology and Psychiatry* 39, no. 1 (1998): 3–27. doi.org/10.1111/1469-7610.00301.

Glenn, Stephen H., Lynn Lott, and Jane Nelsen. *Positive Discipline A–Z: 1001 Solutions to Everyday Parenting Problems.* 3rd ed. New York: Harmony Books, 2007.

GoodTherapy. "Trigger." Accessed March 2020. goodther-apy.org/blog/psychpedia/trigger.

Gongala, Sagari. "Understanding Teenage Behavior Problems and Tips to Handle Them." *MomJunction.* November 8, 2019. momjunction.com/articles/important -teenage-behavioural-problems-solutions_0010084/.

Gowmon, Vince. "6 Ways Children Live in the Present Moment." Accessed April 2020. vincegowmon.com /6-ways-children-live-in-the-present-moment/.

Harvard Health Blog. "The Adolescent Brain: Beyond Raging Hormones." Last modified March 2011. health .harvard.edu/mind-and-mood/the-adolescent-brain -beyond-raging-hormones.

Johnson, Sara B., Robert W. Blum, and Jay N. Giedd. "Adolescent Maturity and the Brain: The Promise and Pitfalls of Neuroscience Research in Adolescent Health Policy." *Journal of Adolescent Health* 45, no. 3 (2009): 216–21. doi.org/10.1016/j.jadohealth.2009.05.016.

Katz, Brigit. "My Child Is a Bully: What Should I Do?" *Child Mind Institute.* Accessed April 2020. childmind.org /article/what-to-do-if-your-child-is-bullying/.

Kristal, Jan. *The Temperament Perspective: Working with Children's Behavioral Styles.* Towson, MD: Brookes, 2005.

———. "Working with Sensitive, Withdrawing Children." *The Highly Sensitive Person.* March 28, 2007. hsperson .com/working-with-sensitive-withdrawing-children/.

Lansbury, Janet. "What to Do about a Toddler Toy Taker." Accessed March 2020. janetlansbury.com/2011/02 /what-to-do-about-a-toddler-toy-taker/.

Making Caring Common Project. "For Families: 5 Tips for Cultivating Empathy." Accessed April 2020. mcc.gse .harvard.edu/resources-for-families/5-tips-cultivating -empathy.

Maxon, Danielle. "Mirroring Your Child's Intense Emotions: 4 Easy Steps." April 7, 2016. daniellemaxon .com/blog/2016/4/6/mirroring-your-childs-intense -emotions.

Mental Health America. "Self-Injury (Cutting, Self-Harm or Self-Mutilation)." Accessed March 2020. mha national.org/conditions/self-injury-cutting-self-harm -or-self-mutilation.

Morin, Amy. "Common Child Behavior Problems and Their Solutions." *Verywell Family.* Last modified September 14, 2019. verywellfamily.com/common-chil d-behavior-problems-and-their-solutions-1094944.

———. "How to Discipline a Child for Spitting." *Verywell Family.* Last modified December 7, 2019. verywellfamily .com/the-best-way-to-discipline-a-child-for-spitting -1094999.

Novotney, Amy. "Parenting That Works." *Monitor on Psychology* 43, no. 9 (2012): 44. apa.org/monitor/2012/10 /parenting.

Patterson, G. R., and M. S. Forgatch. "Predicting Future Clinical Adjustment from Treatment Outcome and Process Variables." *Psychological Assessment* 7, no. 3 (1995): 275–85. doi.org/10.1037/1040-3590.7.3.275.

PBS Kids for Parents. "Practice Mindfulness with Belly Breathing." Accessed April 2020. pbs.org/parents/crafts -and-experiments/practice-mindfulness-with-belly -breathing.

Pegasus: The Magazine of the University of Central Florida. "Your Brain on Music." Accessed March 2020. ucf.edu/pegasus/your-brain-on-music/.

Pincus, Debbie. "When Parents Disagree: How to Parent as a Team." *Empowering Parents.* Accessed April 2020. empoweringparents.com/article/when-parents -disagree-how-to-parent-as-a-team/.

Positive Discipline. "About Positive Discipline." Accessed March 2020. positivediscipline.com/about-positive -discipline.

ProSolutions Training. "Facing the Most Common Problems within Preschool Classrooms." Accessed March 2020. prosolutionstraining.com/resources/articles/ facing-the-most-common-problems-within-preschool -classrooms.cfm.

Rosen, Peg. "Flexible Thinking: What You Need to Know." *Understood.* Accessed April 2020. understood.org /en/learning-thinking-differences/child-learning -disabilities/executive-functioning-issues/flexible -thinking-what-you-need-to-know.

Stephens, Karen. "Parents Are Powerful Role Models for Children." *Parenting Exchange.* Accessed March 2020. easternflorida.edu/community-resources/child -development-centers/parent-resource-library /documents/parents-powerful-role-models.pdf.

Substance Abuse and Mental Health Services Administration. *Trauma-Informed Care in Behavioral Health Services.* Treatment Improvement Protocol (TIP)

Series 57. HHS Publication No. (SMA) 13-4801. Rockville, MD: Substance Abuse and Mental Health Services Administration, 2014.

Sühendan, Er. "Using Total Physical Response Method in Early Childhood Foreign Language Teaching Environments." *Procedia Social and Behavioral Sciences* 93, no. 21 (2013): 1766–68. doi.org/10.1016/j.sbspro.2013.10.113.

TeenMentalHealth.org. "Understanding Self-Injury/Self-Harm." Accessed March 2020. teenmentalhealth.org/understanding-self-injury-self-harm/.

Understood. "Understanding Your Child's Trouble with Organization." Accessed April 2020. understood.org/en/learning-thinking-differences/child-learning-disabilities/organization-issues/understanding-your-childs-trouble-with-organization-and-time-management.

University of Rochester Medical Center. "Understanding the Teen Brain." *Health Encyclopedia.* Accessed March 2020. urmc.rochester.edu/encyclopedia/content.aspx?ContentTypeID=1&ContentID=3051.

Wallace, Marion. "Wallace, Marion." In V. Zeigler-Hill and T. Shackelford (eds.), *Encyclopedia of Personality and Individual Differences.* Cham: Springer, 2016. doi.org/10.1007/978-3-319-28099-8_2157-1.

WebMD. "What Are PTSD Triggers?" Accessed March 2020. webmd.com/mental-health/what-are-ptsd-triggers#1.

Wilson, Catherine. "Understanding Highly Sensitive Children." Accessed March 2020. focusonthefamily.ca /content/understanding-highly-sensitive-children.

WorkLife4You. "Positive Parenting Strategies for the Teenage Years." Accessed March 2020. mftonlineceus .com/ceus-online/ce-difficult-teens/CE-Positive -Parenting-Strategies.pdf.

INDEX

ACKNOWLEDGMENTS

Writing this book was a life-changing journey, one I could not have navigated without the help and dedication of so many.

Thank you to Callisto Media and, more specifically, my editor, Annie Choi, for all your hard work, patience, and impeccable skill.

To my many mentors through the years who have taught me how to be a better educator and parent—thank you.

To my many students along the way, I share this quote from the Talmud: "I have learned much from my teachers, more from my colleagues, and the most from my students."

To my parents, siblings, grandmother, and in-laws, thank you for the unconditional love and support. You assured me I could do it until I began to believe it myself.

And to my incredible husband, thank you for it all: your unwavering faith in me, your patience and understanding, and your constant compassion and selflessness. Thank you for staying up late with me when I had deadlines and for picking up my slack when I needed you to. I love you.

ABOUT THE AUTHOR

 **Yehudis Smith** received her B.A. in English literature from the University of Florida and her M.S.Ed. in early childhood education from Touro College. Yehudis spent 13 years in the classroom, teaching children from 2 to 10 years old, before becoming the owner and operator of Imagined Educational Consulting and Parent Coaching (Imagined-Consulting.com), through which she provides parenting workshops and classes based on the foundations of conscious parenting and speaks regularly as a public and motivational presenter. She also provides professional development services such as teacher coaching, educational consulting, and teacher and administrator workshops. She lives in Parkland, Florida, with her husband and four children.

To learn more about Yehudis and conscious parenting, follow her on Instagram @imaginedcoach or email her at yehudis@imaginedconsulting.com.

9 781647 392505